BROWN
SKIN
AND THE
BEAUTIFUL
FAITH:

A Poet's Reflection

Terry E. Carter

thanks for your support!

BY TERRY E. CARTER

Terry C.

Fisk '80

xulon
PRESS

FOREWORD

I f you are like me and love poetry, you will love *Brown Skin and the Beautiful Faith*. This brother's cadence, rhymes, insights, and mind are amazing; reminds me of Paul Lawrence Dunbar. Serious. I met the author over 20 years ago. Our church ventured into an Arts Ministry, understanding the mandate of Christ to take the good news of God's love into all of the world. We saw that mandate including drama, dance, and poetry. During one of the evening presentations, Terry read some of his poems and so captivated the audience that they stood in applause.

Now I have dabbled a little in writing poems to my wife, and I always get the appreciative hugs and kisses, because she will praise my every effort to romance her. But there's a difference between the "love" scribble of a husband and the wise script of a master. Terry takes poetry to the height it was meant to soar toward, and I for one am honored to call him friend and colleague.

His writing flows out of the deep reservoir of truth and experience within him. As deacons in the church, he and his wife bring a faithfulness of character and integrity into all they do. Their achievements in the arts, his in poetry and hers in dance, have broadened their spheres of influence beyond the walls of the sanctuary. This second project of Terry's is a reflection of this. It is a must read!

Bishop Dr. Gideon Thompson, Founder
Jubilee Christian Church, Boston and Stoughton, MA
Winter, 2014

DEDICATIONS/ ACKNOWLEDGMENTS/ THANKS

B eyond the dedications you may find attached to individual pieces in this 2nd collected volume, I must thank a great many folk who have been part of my continuing journey to poetic maturity, arts ministry, and publication.

As always and with prejudice, I must acknowledge my Lord and Savior Jesus Christ, the true author and finisher of my life. In Him I find the unchallenged source of my gifting and the real reason for sharing those talents with a wider audience.

I also want to thank my most and consistent enthusiastic supporter, my wife Terésa. She is also my "shadow" editor and a disciplined additional set of eyes on this new book, from cover to cover. I also thank my daughter Maya. She has emerged during her collegiate journey as a significant writer and poet in her own right and I look forward to that time when her own book(s) are published and shared with the world. As ever, My mother, Jean Carter and my father, Varnie Carter, have remained my biggest fans. Dad sold a lot of books for me when the first "Brown Skin" was published, so he's definitely written into the new marketing plan. My adopted mom, Roberta Owens-Jones has also been a gracious and genuine supporter and a cherished source of inspiration to my ongoing literary efforts. My Carter Clan and my Owens Clan have all been unfailingly generous in their love for I what I believe and what I write.

More recently, I have taken great inspiration and support from so many others. I will certainly miss someone in the mention, but trust it to my head and not my heart. Bishop Dr. Gideon A. Thompson, Sister "T", Pastor Matt and Pastor Mona of Jubilee Christian Church have all continued to promote the fundamental promise of the arts in effective Christian ministry. In Bishop's foreword to this work, I have been doubly blessed by the trust and respect he's shown as a literature lover and a wise pastoral influence on my life and my gift.

I am so grateful as well for the enthusiastic support the *LYRIC* Poetry Ministry which I've been privileged to direct at Jubilee Christian Church. Much love especially to Yvonne, Sharryn and Zadina, my wonderful *LYRICISTS*...you guys are the best!

In this work especially, I am in a significant rhyme season, lyrically connected to the poets of the Harlem Renaissance and to the Black Arts Movement of Nikki Rosa, Gwendolyn, Amiri, Maya, and Sonia Sanchez. I lament the recent loss of Amiri Baraka, and salute him as a true "revolutionary" in the field of African-American letters. I am also saddened by the passing of Fisk University's beloved son and Professor Emeritus, Dr. Leslie M. Collins, who died at the age of 99 in late February of this year. Dr. Collins, or "Friend" to those who knew him well, was the quintessential scholar of the "Harlem Renaissance" and I learned so much about that period's vibrant literary ascendancy under his instruction. Thank you Friend and may you rest in His gentle peace.

Finally, I want to thank everyone who participated at whatever level in the Kickstarter funding campaign that has underwritten the publication of this new work. I could not have imagined a more rousing rally around my cause. Your spirit and generosity is richly embedded within the rhyme and reason of the Brown Skin universe. I hope each of you sees yourself in something that I've said. I love you all. You know who you are. Enjoy the second leg of the race...

Okay, let the poetry begin. Be blessed.

T.E.C.
Spring 2014

CONTENTS

—BROWN SKIN—

"When you follow in the path of your father,
you learn to walk like him."

ASHANTI PROVERB

For Colored Boys Seeking Heroes
When Father Love Fails

From the brothers who spoke in gold…
bright at times, but also bold—
artistic statements…
the gilded rose on a canvas lament.
The poets simply represent.
The painters make art too…
Bearden, and Langston and Douglas—
art bespoke and true.

From Denzel,
who tossed aside the White Shadow
and became Malcolm X…
He saw Oscar elude, then include
his thespian mastery,
in a rough-cut capacity…
Poitier, Jones and Robeson too—
art bespoke and true.

From the brothers who spoke in red…
spilling their blood
on the battlefields, dead—
casualties of war
and revolutions
not even their own…
From Crispus Attucks to Omar Bradley,
war is hell and war ends sadly.
But courage under fire,
lifts the eagle's wings.

From the Buffalo Soldiers
on the plains, far flung—
Henry O. Flipper and brave Charles Young.
The Tuskegee Airmen
who boldly took flight,
leading white squadrons
into the fight.

Never a sortie of fighters lost—
saving red blood
from the ultimate cost.

From the brothers who spoke in blue—
Miles and Coltrane and Marvin too.
Legacies left on the studio floor,
played like true legends then
shut the front door,
to life and love and music.
Still the music never dies...
Still the legend amplifies,
keeping standard time.

From maestros, musicians
and entertainers—
the Duke and the Count
and their royal retainers.
For life and love and music...
music that never dies.
Jazz and blues and soul—
the legend amplifies.

From the brothers who spoke in brown...
debonair, well-heeled, men-about-town.
In executive boardrooms,
and corporate suites—
Black enterprisers
with strong balance sheets...
John Henry Johnson
and Earl G. Graves...
entrepreneurs,
that made big waves,
laying the bricks
that legacy paves.

From baseball's glorious Negro Leaguers,
brown boys of segregated summers—
when big league clubs enforced the code,
for white men only, the singular road.

Satchel and Oscar, Buck and Pops Lloyd,
Double Duty, Josh –
and "the Rope", Bob Boyd.
Monarchs, Barons, and Stars made do,
until the ascendant
number 42.

From the brothers who spoke in green,
who farmed for their families,
when times were lean...
who scraped an existence
from a sprout or a bean...
Who made it through
the days of Jim Crow...
called nigras, spooks and coons—
prey to the lynch mobs
and rabid goons,
the hooded marauders...
in the heat of the night.

For colored boys to whom
the label "nigger" is not a joke—
for hi-topped, hoodied white boys,
hopped-up on Jay-Z, Jag and beer,
to call each other and brown boys too.
Brother-man don't you hear?
Yo, that word ain't cool.
That word is a hateful tool.
Real brothers as a rule—
won't touch this.

From the brothers who speak in purple—
The royal of faith is a dark violet hue...
Jakes and Bismark to name a few,
Gideon Thompson in Boston too.
Fred Hammond sings the gospel story...
while Marvin Sapp brings down
that heavenly glory.
Israel Houghton, a friend of God...
think it not strange, peculiar, or odd.
God sends His word

through men of spirit,
and men of truth.

For little colored boys with hopes and dreams—
look to the Lord with your plans and schemes.
He is Father to the fatherless,
mender of broken hearts...
balm in Gilead,
and joy of your salvation.
He will shoulder your burden
and be the single set
of footprints in the sand,
as He carries you along the shore
of life's disappointments and despair.

From the men who speak in pink,
heroes, much in love we think...
with moms whose cancer
shrinks their hope,
and sisters they help to deal and cope,
and wives at the end of their fragile rope.
They help to tell the tale,
keep up the fight,
promote the cause—
Check's in the mail.

Such is the rainbow for little colored boys—
seeking fathers and heroes,
not candy and toys...
Seeking fathers and heroes
that don't cut and run,
when the battle gets heated
and the hard times come.

Such is the rainbow for little colored boys—
seeking fathers and heroes,
not pimps, wimps and decoys...
Seeking fathers and heroes
that lead honest lives,
that honor their mothers
and pray with their wives.

Gold and red and brown and green—
this is the rainbow they've not yet seen.
Purple and blue and even pink—
a different rainbow
than one might think.

Barbie Doesn't Live Here

I heard my sister say,
I'll never fit in a size two.
I got hips and a booty
and so do you.
Why you so stressed
'bout your BMI?
The brothers like
that ample thigh.
Barbie doesn't live here...
No aquiline nose.
No perfect toes.
No designer clothes.
Macy's won't call you
for a photo-shoot.
Lane Bryant's on sale...
So you better scoot.
Don't worry a bit
'bout hitting the gym.
He drinks whole milk.
He doesn't like skim.
Barbie doesn't live here...
No teensy-weensy waist.
No food that has no taste.
No facial with blue paste.
Those skinny broads
in the magazines—
those ain't women.
They're barely teens.
You crave your mama's
seven-up cake,
Southern fried chicken,
and cheesy-mac bake.
Barbie doesn't live here...
No collagen lips.
No tucks and no nips.
No two-inch nail tips.
You got curves like

your Auntie Pearl.
Who always tells you,
g'on and get it girl!
You're a healthy size ten
with a sassy strut,
a nicely-turned calf,
and a glorious butt.
Barbie doesn't live here...
No silicon boobs.
No liposuction.
No needles or tubes.
No breast reduction.
All of those dolls,
they look the same...
just different outfits
and corny names.
So let's not even
fantasize—
'bout a size two figure,
and some baby blue eyes.
Like I been sayin',
Barbie doesn't live here...
Not at this address.
Not in this vicinity.
Not in the neighborhood.
Not in my reality.
I ain't mad at her.
She's actually a cute white chick.
And that pink corvette was hot.

HBCU

The Freedmen's Bureau and other concerns,
provided for that
which a black man yearned.
Degrees which only coloreds could earn...
Classrooms where only Negros could learn...
At times, in the places where crosses burned.
Started in churches
and normal schools—
mindful of bigots,
haters, and fools.

Money raised in a thousand ways...
from collection buckets,
to Jubilee days...
Singers that traveled
all over the globe—
returning their proceeds
to build beyond probes...

Probes of family pedigree.
Probes of social registry.
Probes of right ethnicity.
Probes of privileged legacy.

Education and a chance to hope—
at places where brown skin could easily cope.
DuBois even called them the talented tenth.
They'd never give up, never relent...
Worth every penny of scholarship spent—
every tin nickel, every red cent.

Bootstraps and philanthropy,
character and integrity...
often Christian fellowship,
was added to their college trip.
When no other school or institution,
would honor Black men with resolution
of Jim Crow's racial destitution.

The army would come to integrate
college in the Southern state,
beyond racism, exclusion or hate...
yet couldn't make the road quite straight.

Thus, negro schools would elevate—
with only the heart to educate....
with only a mind to innovate...
with wisdom to inoculate.

Tiny rooms or ivy-clad walls—
a vision and a duty called,
scholars and teachers in hallowed halls
to act in the interests
of brown-skinned brothers,
sons and heirs of Negro mothers,
kin of far less fortunate others.

Great are the names of those hallowed halls.
Long is the roster that history calls.
More than a few are listed here...
Did you go to this one—
or the one over there?

Fisk, Tuskegee and Tougaloo—
Spelman, the "House", and Hampton too...
Howard, the land grant in greater DC,
Two Lincolns, a Langston, and A & T...
St. Aug's, Lane, and Benedict College,
dispensing historical brown-skinned knowledge.

Dozens of quality institutions...
legacy-bound by black resolutions—
there for the daughters of slavery's pain,
there for the sons of freedom's refrain.

The United Negro College Fund,
scholarships given, victories won...
"The mind is a terrible thing to waste."
Black college life,
here's a bit of a taste—

Sorority rush and fraternity row...
Many would pledge, many said no.
Deltas and Kappas and AKA's,
Nasty Q dawgs and their scandalous ways...
Alpha Phi Alpha, the black and gold,
summoned the best, both bright and bold.
Zetas, Phi Betas, and Gamma Rhos...
Many would pledge, many said no.

Campus steppers and beautiful queens—
scholar-athletes arrived on the scene.
They knew our struggle.
They heard our voice.
Even as times changed,
they made this choice.

Not always perfect,
they made mistakes.
Still they must do,
whatever it takes—
to hold up a wonderful legacy,
extending the black college family tree.

So many tales these walls could tell,
of luminaries that answered the bell.
They rose above a nation's bid,
to keep its black sons and daughters hid.

Folks with the soul of poetry,
words that set the brown mind free...
heroes for all the world to see,
Thurgood Marshall and Nikki G.
Oprah, Ralph Ellison,
and W.E.B.

Ida B. Wells and
James Weldon Johnson
shared this bloodline too—
rising above the hate and pain
to write for folks like you.

There were special brothers
with special names,
like Langston Hughes
and "Chappie" James.
They called Doug Williams "Quarterblack"—
a Super Bowl winning quarterback...
He was the first of a talented pair.
Alcorn State gave us Steve McNair.

Sisters created great stories too.
Bessie Coleman majestically flew,
from Langston College
to the skies of blue.
A female pilot, who lit the lamp—
emblazoned on a postage stamp.
And before Serena took Wimbledon,
FAMU's Althea also won.

Alex Haley created deep "Roots",
while Andrew Young wore power suits.
More heroes than fit in the lines of this poem—
Black college seeds, in rich, fertile loam.

Jerry Rice and Rosa Parks...
One called the GOAT, the other the spark.
He was the NFL's all-time best.
She stood up to the Jim Crow test—
that started a Civil Rights symphony,
and led to the nation's epiphany.
Joined by James Farmer and Benjamin Hooks—
all of them schooled in black college books.

More than a brown-skinned brother can know—
like Wilma Rudolph...
now that girl could go.
Walter Payton, the one they called "Sweetness"...
but still so far from a list of completeness.

I'll not be able to name them all here—
such greatness salting the atmosphere.

Perhaps I'll end with this worthy one—
Hampton's Booker T. Washington.
Much is included in his legacy,
like starting the Institute, Tuskegee.

Such are the sons...
and such are the daughters...
that crossed the burning sands,
and sailed the danger waters.
I wrote this poem without such risk.
My craft, like many, was honed at Fisk.

We did it for community—
so many others too...
creating a singular unity.
We do it today—
at the HBCU.

I Just Want to Be Black for a Day

Coltrane's cool…with no demise —
Billie's voice and Iman's eyes…
Herschel Walker's monster thighs…
I just want to be Black for a day.

A brotha's hug and some secret dap —
Gospel riffs and a holy soul clap…
Gregory Hines and the art of tap…
I just want to be Black for a day.

Shiny black Benzo on 22's —
Grandmaster Flash, 'bout to light a fuse…
MJ and Scottie's Bulls don't lose…
I just want to be black for a day.

I don't want Denny's to refuse me service,
and blue-haired matrons getting' nervous.
Can't I just act like a caramel tourist,
and be black for just a day?

With the looks of Beyoncé and the luck of Jay-Z —
Is that so wrong to want to be ?
Aunt Oprah's juice on cable TV…
That would be black like me.

I'd have the talent of Quincy Jones —
and be funny like Cosby with shows of my own.
MTV "Cribs" would visit my home,
if I could be black for a day.

The po-lice would never profile me.
Trayvon and DJ, I'd never be.
Strange fruit hangin' from a tree,
that's not my black for a day.

I'd like to tan and never burn —
Hang with Lebron and dunk to earn…

Money would never be a concern.
That is my black for a day.

Not Compton, or Watts, or Cabrini Green—
Bed-Stuy and Newark are also too mean.
I'd have to live where it's gated and clean,
if I could be black for a day.

Church with Jakes at the Potter's House—
or Bishop Thompson at Jubilee South…
Praisin' the Lord and the Holy Ghost …
Amen. I'm just black for the day.

Got the job, 'cause the boss insisted—
They need some diversity, don't get it twisted.
Usually brown skin gets 'em black-listed.
But not when I'm black for a day.

I'd be the most likely one to succeed.
My chocolate hue would not impede.
My soulful strut would take the lead.
I'm cool when I'm black for a day.

I'd get admitted to Harvard or Yale—
and never have to think of jail…
no phone calls, begging for my bail.
That's not my black for a day.

In twenty-four hours, I'd give it back—
leaving the 'hood for my whiter track.
I'm hoping they'll cut me a little slack.,
on the day I choose to be black.

I know I can't lose with the skin I'm in—
in the place where black folks never win.
The curse of race is such a sin.
I just want to be black for a day.

Jubilee Voices

Bathed in glory
by crowned heads of state...
traveling bards,
propelled by the fates.
Symbols of blackness
and whitewashed fears—
sang of the Negro's
bondage and tears.
Songs of the coming Jubilee...
This is what freedom
means to me.

Saluting the Fisk University Jubilee Singers,
Summer 2011

Invisible Women, Invisible Men

We run this race in the heat of the day.
Yet they don't see us —
when we walk this way.

Freedom Riders in the deepest South,
the death threat passed by word of mouth...
Camelot had to be dragged —
kickin', scratchin' and screamin'
to Charleston, Atlanta and Birmingham.

Mammies took care of your
blonde-haired babies —
while you labeled their own
pick-a-ninnies and nigra chiles'.

LBJ was sickened by the slights —
so he surrendered to the power of light...
to the power of what's right...
to the bills he'd sign despite —
the ridicule, the malevolence
and the loss of incumbency,
and certain coronation,
beyond Camelot.

Invisible Women, invisible men...
they didn't want to see us then.
Rosa would sit,
to whisper a choice.
But few would choose
to hear her voice.
Medgar, then Malcolm, then Martin
would grow...
but bullets would fly
to lay each man low.

Still—
this kind of violence,
sees no vow of silence...
And even the chosen
of Camelot falls.
First Jack, then Bobby
in rapid succession—
a country divided,
by race and rejection.

Invisible daughters, invisible sons—
identity searched for, but not yet won,
like stories by Zora and Ralph Ellison...
the peaceable kingdom, not yet come.
Wounds that time has not yet healed—
Perhaps to be black,
is to know how this feels.

Ridin' Up Front

Can't do it.
Don't even ask me, Black...
It's a bus.
But I ain't ridin' in the back.
Youngbloods—
they ain't got no idea,
of how long
we had to ride in the rear.
In the lazy South,
American apartheid.
The law of the land
was stratified...
Seats up front
unoccupied,
yet a pregnant brown girl
can't sit and ride.
Elders, toddlers,
just didn't matter.
And don't let 'em hear
no race talk or chatter.
Red neck drivers
would put us out.
But y'all don't know
what I'm talkin' 'bout.

Then along came
courageous Rosa Parks—
tired and weary,
but full of sparks.
Took a seat
in the first few rows,
seeking not chaos,
but simple repose.
Think them whites
heard what she was sayin'?
Hell no...
and them crackers

for sure wasn't playin'...
Jailed up Miss Rosa
without dignity,
commending her acts
to our history.
But you
don't have no gratitude—
no pride in self,
just attitude.
You make your way
to the back of the bus.
You drink and smoke
and holler and cuss.
You say, it's your prerogative.
You say, it's just the way you live.
You just don't get it.
You just don't care.
So cavalier...
so unaware.

But I can't do it.
Don't even ask me, Black...
It's a bus.
But I ain't ridin' in the back.
Free seats up front—
that's' for me.
I'm diggin'
Miss Rosa's
legacy.

The Warming of Other Suns

They made their way north in caravans,
to cities of industry, jobs and hope.
Sometimes with just the clothes on their backs—
they ran from the klansmen and racist attacks.
They'd witnessed lynchings.
They'd dined on Jim Crow.
And thus, the South would provoke them to go,
in search of other suns.

Warmer suns.

Perhaps not the body, but warming the soul—
made whole, in Detroit, Chicago and Harlem, USA.
The same tracks that led them underground,
they rode these rails to live unbound.
They'd all share-cropped.
Now they whistle-stopped...
looking for the land of opportunity.
They searched for other suns.

Brighter suns.

Bright beyond the reach of 'Bama woods,
where bitter fruit hung on blackened trees.
Light that led to broader streets and brown-skinned dreams—
bright like speckled trout in country streams.
They'd lived out fear in shotgun shacks...
and had to watch each other's backs.
Now Southern stars would fade
before these Northern suns.

Rising Suns.

Rising like the smoke from factory stacks,
where brown hands fashioned and fabricated
American things for the new community—
whose open doors suggested they were free.

They'd sit in classrooms learning, black and white.
They'd pray in church together, in God's sight.
None would say that they had truly won,
only that they'd found a warmer sun.

Only that they'd found a warmer sun.

Within These Walls

I won't feign any guise of innocence.
I won't claim any special ignorance.
I'll simply beg forgiveness, and then yield.
Yield to the sentence I must serve...
Yield to the rod of correction...
Yield to the world of walls,
which has become my home.

You won't write letters every day.
You won't come visit like you say.
You will forget and turn away.
Away from our family embarrassment...
Away from the stain I represent...
Away from the brick, the steel and cement,
which closes in my home.

The wolves around me salivate.
These predators, weakness anticipate.
There is only persecution here, and hate.
Hate fuels the fires that burn inside...
Hate fuels the rage of fratricide...
Hate fuels the rape, the violent tide...
which flows within my home.

My path to freedom, I can't see.
My demons so beset and torture me.
My God, I sometimes ask, "How can He be?"
Be compassion that forgives my sin...
Be perfected grace my soul to win...
Be the silent calm which stills the din...
which echoes in my home.

Father, hear my muffled cry of pain.
Father, be the voice of my refrain.
Father, heed my prayer to love again.
Within these walls, I seek rebirth.
Within these walls, my arms stretch forth...
Within these walls, a star points north.
Perhaps true north,
which leads me to my home.

—REVIVAL—

"Let love and faithfulness never leave you.
Bind them around your neck.
Write them on the tablet of your heart."

PROVERBS 3:3–HOLY BIBLE (NIV)

Revival

Evangelists will come—
and they will go...
entreating the faithful
to let their passion show.
Crying for
the called out ones
to let their vision grow—
Preaching so
the lost and strayed,
may enter in and know—
Know Him who gathers
the wandering sheep,
and covers the restless
with peaceful sleep,
and fathoms the order
of mysteries deep,
and shows us His promises,
ever to keep.

Who Loves Like This?

Two days of labor, harder than granite…
The baby is coming—no she didn't plan it.
Too young and foolish to care for herself,
these were the cards that the enemy dealt.

She must've cried most every night—
frozen by fear at a young girl's plight…
frozen by choices she thought meant love…
frozen by voices not sent from above.

A double epidural birth—
it felt like God had moved the earth.
A shaking rocked her youthful womb.
The baby kicked to make more room.

The child came in the dead of night—
colic and croup and couldn't eat right.
Kept her bound and so uptight,
she must've cried most every night.

Motherhood, mixed with joy and pain—
like Frankie sang, "sunshine and rain"…
But mama loves this baby boy,
although she thinks he's just a toy.

Still, God Himself would see this done—
and yet anoint this unplanned son.
Soon he'd be a special man,
to a frightened mama without a plan.

Who can speak of love like this…
a beloved son and a chocolate kiss?
Who can fathom such a wonder…
with all of the pain she labored under?

He's preaching now, all over the world—
Jehovah's banner in him unfurled.
His mama goes along to tell,
the story of their flight from hell.

She speaks of a savior who lives in glory—
and moved each piece in her life's story.
She speaks of a Father who loves her soul,
and gave her a purpose, complete and whole.

Now, she alone can testify—
of how He would not let her die.
She alone can give account,
of how she drank from grace's fount.

He brought her to a life of bliss.
He is the One that loves like this.

Symphony

The maestro steps to the stage.
He taps his baton a time or two.
Musicians are anxious to play—
each with a job to do.
The concert hall says Symphony...
a place that produces fidelity.
Lyrical, rhythmic melody—
played with well-tuned mastery.

The preacher approaches the altar.
He picks up the microphone.
The choir has set the atmosphere,
and worship establishes tone.
The Man of God says Symphony...
a people walking in unity,
total agreement and clarity—
a kinship of faith, hope and charity.

The servant embraces her gifting.
She teaches, or dances, or prays.
Her soul and spirit are one in faith.
Her witness embraces His ways.
The servant's heart says Symphony...
reflecting His purpose consistently,
righteous, redemptive reality—
embracing the vision of destiny.

The lamb reveals its loss and pain.
It struggles, and stumbles and falls.
Its lonely and wayward spirit yearns,
to hear its shepherd's call.
The lost and alone crave Symphony.
They long to hear His melody.
Salvation, and grace and liberty—
the path made straight in victory.

The church encounters the world,

growing beyond doubt and pride...
Establishing faith in the mission fields,
equipping the faithful inside.
The house of God says Symphony...
one body, Christ-like, unceasingly.
Matured by travail and humility —
Walking by faith, and shared history.

The pastor asks these questions —
Are you really ready to play?
Did you bring your proper instrument?
Did you practice your part today?
The gift of God is Symphony...
Ordered in wonderful mystery —
created in perfect complexity,
elevating all of humanity.

The shofar blast is heard —
and borders come crashing down.
The church without walls is revealed...
and the city becomes hallowed ground.
The gifted response says Symphony...
a dark world's hope for harmony.
The Father, the Son, and the Holy Ghost —
Symphony summons the Lord of Hosts.

Dedicated to JCC, 2014, the year of Symphony...
January, 2014

Without A Test

No testimony
without a test—
Leave to Jesus
and let it rest.
A feather-like burden ,
a glove-soft yoke—
take in His grace.
Let it bathe you...
just soak.

Never a novel
without a story—
yield to His passion,
find peace
beyond worry.
Look to the Cross
and the Chief Cornerstone.
Find the Good Shepherd,
no lamb left alone.

Each revelation,
has its own tell.
Knock on His door.
He'll answer the bell.
Salvation assurance,
an anchor for life—
give Him a chance.
He'll banish all strife.

No testimony
without a test—
hide in the Savior's
warm, sheltered nest.
The Son of Mankind
alive in the world.
Give Him your praise,
as His banner unfurls.

Do That Dance of Faith

Do that dance of faith you do,
when the spirit of the Lord
is moving you.

Stomp your feet and clap your hands.
The choir shouts—
Worship demands...
He's watching too.

Wave those flags and glory hoops,
in sheer delight
and whirling loops...
This thing is new.

Before you're done,
the dance you lead
will make the angels intercede...
and bring breakthrough.

Do that dance of faith that makes
the children smile.
The colors and the movement,
and the rhythmic style—
move us up and down...
the crowded aisle.

We'll press to follow you,
whenever you do—
that wondrous dance of faith...
We'll do it too.

Dedicated to Eagle Terésa and the Spirit and Truth Dance Ministry of JCC
Winter 2013

Small in Your Own Eyes

It was in the book...plain as day—
but I, could not see it.
How then, could I be it?

How not to serve
the greed of masters?
How to join hands
with the praisers and fasters?

I had important things to do—
places to go—
people to meet...
No time to bow down
at my savior's feet.

But I heard it said
in an island tongue,
"Small up yourself"
to dwell among—
the righteous of
the Father.

Your bold intentions
and constant aggressions,
constrain you to
the corridors of pride.
But God resists such vanity
and watches from
the window...
He's outside.

Can't you see
the certain terror of the night—
heir to death because,
you can't be
humble in His sight.

The wise one used to say,
"Small up yourself."
Blessed are the meek—
with Godly wealth.

Boastful, haughty words—
and prideful ways,
reduce the Father's
number for your days.

It's written in the book,
sure as sunrise.
Daughter, son—
be small,
in your own eyes.

Facebook Post #3

Sunday...aaaahhh!

Blessed, healed, and delivered through another week.

Give the Savior some dap and say that you knew

He had you all along...

Because he did.

He died to prove it.

What greater love is there than this?

Now we are joint heirs to the whole nine,

cattle on a thousand hills, many mansions, unmerited favor...

the whole nine.

So go to your Daddy's house and give Him a big shout...

"To God be the glory!"

That's what I'm talkin' 'bout.

Facebook Post #4

The loss of our sobriety,

the dangers of notoriety,

the scourge of tainted piety,

and menaces to society...

Why won't we let Him set us free?

Jesus, the Saviour, can set the world free.

Qualified Salvation

Can't I just do some of it?
Why must I do all of it?
Do I have to walk in it?
Do I have to talk of it?
Can't I just fake it,
'til I'm able to make it?

How about the gift of grace —
they always wave before my face?
They say your love will just forgive,
each and every lie I live.
Talkin' 'bout a "made-up mind"…
what if that's too hard to find?

Can't I just be who I am?
I like a little glitz and glam.
I like to hang out at the club,
with a shot of jack and a glass of bub'.
I like that "bad boy" look I get,
when I jump at sin,
without a net.

I'm saved.
I made it plain and clear…
for the pastor and my mom to hear.
I took a class and joined a cell.
I answered when you rang the bell.

But can't I pass on all these rules?
I like some bling, some swag, some jewels.
It's hard to floss and still pay tithes…
I got a note on both my rides.

Is Jesus looking all the time —
judging me on every crime?
Am I losing points for pride —
anger, lust and faith denied?

Will my faults push me outside,
from His grace disqualified?

Can't I just do some of it?
Why must I do all of it?
Do I have to walk in it?
Do I have to talk of it?
Can't I just fake it,
'til I'm able to make it?

Maybe I can just give up—
the little wafer and the cup...
nix the monthly consecration,
and live a qualified salvation.

His Word Is Spoken Here

The fingers are snappin',
snap, snap, snap—
Those in the know will
clap, clap, clap.
Jazz to set the atmosphere...
His word is spoken here.

There's talk of prophets,
Isaiah and such...
Destiny's call
to the Master's touch.
No hard liquor, wine or beer...
His word is spoken here.

The poet's are clever
and lyrically sound—
meter and rhyme
to wisdom profound...
No cursing, hate, or fear,
His word is spoken here.

The fellowship is tight and sweet.
The drummers tap out
a rhythmic beat.
We hear the message,
loud and clear.
His word is spoken here.

Place Your word Lord,
in my mouth.
Let me speak it—
North and South.
Let them come from far and near.
Your word is spoken here.

Fill me with
Your poetry.

Let Your vision
flow through me.
Hold me close and dear.
I'll speak Your word right here.

—EAGLES—

"An army of sheep led by a lion can defeat
an army of lions led by a sheep."

GHANAIAN PROVERB

Legacy No. 42

His number forever immortalized,
in all of the game's hallowed grounds...
Jackie pushed baseball's history,
beyond baseball's out of bounds.

The courage not to fight the man,
he fit right into Branche Rickey's plan.
Changing the tortured soul of the game,
he made a nation remember his name.

Up from the fabled Negro Leagues —
first to cross over and plant the seed...
Refusing to bow or tolerate,
a second class citizen's usual fate.

Made his toughest critics see,
that baseball needed diversity.
Paved the way for others too —
Newk' and Campy to name a few.

A legend, a leader, a firebrand,
so fleet of foot, so quick to stand...
up to the taunts and epithets...
revised the sport with no regrets.

Soon all-colored teams would fade,
into the progress his courage made.
Monarchs, Eagles, and Cuban X Giants,
would heed the call to end their alliance.

Following Jackie over the line,
baseball's black glory redefine.
Mays and Aaron would reinvent —
with number 42's precedent.

But no one before and no one since...
could ever do much more to convince,
the white man to open the gates to the game—
allowing the black man to share in its fame.

We owe this man such gratitude,
for changing the game's angry attitude.
His number forever saluted—
his legacy hence, undisputed.

Malcolm Knew

He knew that "Malcolm Little"
would ultimately not be enough man,
to support either his mission
or his methods.

He knew that black pride,
in Omaha, and in East Lansing
would be a death sentence for him too—
if he stayed.

He knew that the good times
in Boston and in Harlem—
the liquor and the drugs and the high livin'
wouldn't last forever.

Through Earl and Marcus and Ella,
he knew.
After ten years on the streets and in the joint—
he knew.

He knew that the Nation of Islam
was the sea change he sought
to become a whole man,
proud and defiant.

He knew that compromise
did not suit this "Ex-Coloured Man"...
and that the "Little" name,
was a leash to his past, not a link to his future.

He knew that he was a leader—
that men would hearken unto him.
He knew they'd embrace the movement,
cleaving to its promise of revolution and change.

Beyond Jim Crow and the Klu Kluxers,
he knew.
Through Elijah Muhammad and the Holy Quran,
he knew .

He knew that while Malcolm Little,
had only been up for the party—
Malcolm X,
was down for the struggle.

He knew that peaceful coexistence,
was a luke-warm retort to lynchings.
He knew that the path of Gandhi and King,
was not his particular thing.

He knew that "Power concedes nothing
without a demand."
He knew that "by any means necessary,"
Black folks must throw off the yoke of oppression.

Still, power often made simple men, simply blind.
As a practical matter, he knew that
Islam's most fervent message was one of peace.
In spiritual awakening, he knew.

He knew that while Malcolm X,
had been down for the struggle—
El-Hajj Malik El-Shabazz,
was up for the enlightenment.

He knew in his epiphany,
they could no longer bear his voice.
He embraced the human family,
and they couldn't respect his choice.

He dreamed of a "bloodless revolution..."
But he knew that the gunmen would come.
He dreamed of Pan-African peace and unity.
But he knew that he'd never see it.

In the brilliance of the Hajj, he knew.
In the solace of his prayers, he knew.
In the well of his spirit's renewal, he knew.

In redemption and release—
Malcolm knew.

In memory of El-Hajj Malik El-Shabazz,
October 2012

Martin's Wake

In the rural manse and the urban sprawl,
he left a love of harmony.
He left the hope of dreams.
He left a land awakened to
the song of diversity and
the soul of the rainbow.

Honoring the memory of Dr. Martin Lither King, Jr.
January 15, 2013

An Ode To The Senator

From out of Demopolis, awash in Red clay —
came a Boston icon some poets say.
He sang a little doo-wop back in the day,
with brothers and cousins, crooning hey, hey, heyyy...

Mutton-chop sides and a sculpted 'fro,
this Malcolm-type brother was down for the show.
Loved his mama, sweet Mary Alice —
got into stuff, but without any malice.

Loved his sisters, Shirley and 'Bert —
all of them raised on Demopolis dirt.
With L.J., Joe, Hank, Johnny and Rob...
came up to Boston, for hope and a job.

From the 'Pan, to the Dot', then up to the 'Bury —
stood out among the ordinary.
Liked to debate the affairs of the land,
could go there and take a principled stand.

Became a new voice for the common man,
then a voice in the House with a solid plan.
Became a strong voice for down-trodden masses,
then made Senators get up off their...sssshhhh —

Y'all know where this poet must go.
Can't say the word, so act like you know.
First to call out "the wealthy elite"
a notion Obama would later repeat.

Taking to task the one per cent,
who take all the credit and don't pay no rent.
This Senator, like a black light lamp,
would light up the flaws in the white folks camp.

Always a stand on health education—
A singular voice for black reparations—
Adept at creating impact legislation—
Always demanding the best from our nation.

Stood tall beside Boston's leading men,
Landsmark, Mel King and Bolling back when—
a Mayor named White, watched Louise Day Hicks
and Southie boys with bats and sticks.

William brought the fight to the streets—
no hint of surrender, no hint of retreat.
He fought with his head, his heart and his feet—
victories many, but few real defeats.

Fought to keep black brothers healthy—
Created wealth, while others got wealthy—
Knew how to do things, big things, you feel me.
Knew how to do things, good things, to heal me.

A green revolution in Abuja—
promoting clean solar in Africa.
Community housing in Roxbury—
Mandela Homes, an LLP.

Created SOMBWA for Black business aid—
Owens made sure some brothers got paid.
The Urban League to the NAACP—
looking for ways to set folks free...

From the New School for Children to Project JESI—
looking for ways to set folks free...
The Founding Director of H.E.L.P.—
looking for ways to set folks free...

Dedicated funding for AIDS/HIV—
looking for ways to set folks free...
Schooling our kids in Black history—
looking for ways to set folks free...
Thirty million bucks to build RCC—
looking for ways to set folks free.

From out of Demopolis, can you believe,
what this country boy would grow to achieve.
On these Boston streets he became quite a fella,
and can still hold a tune, no doubt acapella.

From Beacon Hill to Hazleton Street—
Bill Owens, a man you may want to meet.

Honoring Senator William Owens, Sr.
of Boston, Massachusetts
Christmas, 2011

My Daddy's Hands

His were the hands that
were just a bit afraid to
hold my newborn baby girl.
She was so very tiny...

Plaster and lime,
over distance and time—
had made his skin
so rough and unyielding.

Still, the looks said love...
and the looks said he was proud.
And the looks said,
that's my gran'baby.

One time, when he was
on the job with my brother...
a piano fell on my brother's leg.
His were the hands that pushed
great weigh aside—
and carried a whimpering boy
tenderly to safety...
no curses, no recriminations.

My daddy love basketball...
and my brother was pretty good
in high school.
I can remember Pop
clapping at the game and smiling broadly—
made me wish I could play too.
But God made me good at other things,
and Pop clapped for me too.
Oh, how I loved
those clapping hands.

I loved those hammering hands...
and those tiling hands,

and those plastering hands too.
I loved those praying hands,
that took us to church...
and taught us how
to love the Lord,
with our own hands held high,
and pointed to the hills...
from whence came our help.

They were the same hands,
that pulled my mama close
for a smooch...
and spanked me and my sibling's butts,
when we didn't do
as we were told.

They were the same hands,
that held the wheel,
for what seemed like
days at a time...
on those hot summer road trips
to sleepy Carlisle, PA
and deep, dark Mississippi.

Those hands built our home
and paid our bills...
and put me through college—
Fisk University.
He clapped real hard
when I graduated,
Summa Cum Laude
and Phi Beta Kappa.

My baby girl's
grown now...
She's in college too.
Mine are the hands
she speaks of now.
Mine are the hands
"pushing the plow."

I hope she'll remember
the things I've built,
the embraces I've given...
the miles I've driven,
and even the rod
I've not spared,
in raising the child.

I hope she remembers—
the way I remember...
those rough, unyielding hands.

My Daddy's hands.

Presidential Lament

You're trying to beat
this good man down...
and bloody his head
with a thorny crown...
You blame him for all your omissions,
reviling his cherished positions.

Does this make you principled?
Does this make you true?
No, this makes you childish.
And this makes you rude.

Everyone—
around the world,
sees this for what it is.
Contempt and disruption
by diffident men,
the conscience of leaders hid.

Does this make you proud?
Does this make you good?
No, this is scorched earth—
but not in your 'hood.

You've called him liar,
and foreigner.
You've questioned his faith,
his spirit to blur.
You've created fear and distrust...
in the land of free and the just.

This makes you seem
repugnant and crass...
lacking in substance, lacking in class.
It doesn't seem wrong to call you the ass...
Stubborn, stupid, obstinate
certain to procrastinate,

no compromise and always late—
to recognize authority…
to temper your temerity…
to speak with more civility…
and act with no hostility.

Plagued by arch conservatives—
this isn't how Americans live.
We use the term respect—
to name who we elect.

A three-tier system of government,
demands that leaders represent.
And show the world we honor he—
who leads our cause with dignity.
There's no room for malice, no room for hate.
We sent you there to legislate.

Men of honor can disagree,
without condemning the family.
Men of good intentions all—
should never let our champion fall.

We the people, were confident,
our wishes you'd all implement…
And yet you strive for nothing less,
than cursing all he seeks to bless.
Here is the thing to understand—
he's President of all the land.

Don't curse him or lament…
Barack Obama, our President.

Simply Langston

Poet colossus—
he strode through literature's pantheon,
with unabashed negritude
and genial swagger.
Adorned his head
with a laureate's crown
and declared—
that God had made
a black bard
and bid him sing.

Harlem lion—
he storified Simple and glorified laughter,
to the people of slavery's wake
and tragedy's wind.
Carried a tray
and served up
brown, sweet cordials,
bittersweet rhythms,
and the blues—
on ice.

Renaissance giant—
he embodied the soul of the black aesthete.
To the dandies in the Dark Tower,
and the dancers at the Savoy...
Lent lyrics to the beat,
and rhyme to the reason—
that black was beauty,
that black was worthy,
that the black man's
season had come.

Simply Langston—
he saved his brother's sorrow songs.
For the porters on the trains,
and sharecroppers planting grains...

he bathed American dreams
in African hues,
in alternate views,
and the majesty
of a history
all our own.

Soweto Song: For Madiba

The Boers declared Apartheid's rule—
in seizing Cape Town's precious jewel.
But rebels with a noble cause,
would snatch the land from Botha's jaws.

Fighting for the Kaffir boys, Soweto born and bound,
never to know a life beyond the township's separate ground.
Fighting for the revolution, you took it to the streets—
equality your solution, through victories and defeats.

With Tambo and the ANC,
you changed the course of history—
inciting men to take up arms,
and put their lives at risk of harm.

They prosecuted you—
condemning you for life...
stolen from your family,
expanding civil strife.
No jail cell could contain—
the arc of your ascent...
even Robben Island's
cold steel and cement.

Your sacrifice of bondage
spanned ten thousand days.
A long, hard walk to freedom showed
the greatness of your ways.

The struggle's cost is always high.
You took no solace there.
Yet Biko's fall and Sharpeville's cry,
Would make a world aware.

You suffered violence and authored force—
though peace would be your final course.
You taught the world to lift its voice,
demanding a democratic choice.

Madiba, Tata of our land,
for you we held the whiter hand.
Xhosa, Thembu, royal prince,
none but you could then convince —
a racist host to loose its grasp
and open freedom's golden clasp.

So rest in honor; repose in grace.
Soweto smiles on your sleeping face.

For Nelson Rolihlahla Mandela, Statesman, Prince and Peacemaker.
Rest in Peace...
December 5, 2013

On His Broad Shoulders...

On his broad shoulders rest
the most difficult decisions one man can make.
How to shield a sovereign democracy
from the terrorist threat and the zeal of hate.
How to share the wealth of the nation's vast riches
with the dense pockets of poverty that exist beside
the lavish gated communities
and mansions of affluence.
How to preserve the once-proud middle class
that so many citizens aspire to.
How to heal the breach
in the civility of public discourse.

On his broad shoulders rest
the most weighty of man-made responsibilities...
feeding the poor and hungry...
comforting the bereaved...
giving hope to the dispirited...
energizing the apathetic...
reconnecting the disenfranchised...
raising the tide that lifts all boats...
navigating through the storms of strife and violence
in distant theaters of war.

On his broad shoulders rests
the pride of a people once enslaved...
the Proverbs and Psalms
that the prophet's gave...
the promise to all
of a Christ that saves...
the abiding faith
that all people crave, and
the path to forgiveness
we've yet to pave.

On his broad shoulders rests
the journey of leading society...

the promise of future prosperity...
protecting the best in our history...
preserving the health of our legacy...
promoting the strength of diversity
restoring a sense of integrity..
to all things uniquely American...
wherever they may have been born.

On his broad shoulders rests
the sacrifice of our forefathers...
the earnest intent of the framers...
the pillars of public service...
the perfect pitch of diplomacy...
the consistent retort to tyranny...
the affirmation of human dignity...
the rallying cry of our unity...
the fragrant refrain of posterity...
the amber waves of grain and
proof that our flag is still there.

Draped around his broad
and magnificent shoulders,
our flag is still there.

**For President Barack Obama, the leader of the free world
and the hope of nations yet to be born.**
October, 2012

—JAZZ JEWELS—

"Black or White, the footprints left in the dirt are the same."

AFRICAN PROVERB

The Tragic Night of Lady Day

Gardenia poised in hot pressed curls...
the soulful lyrics, her voice unfurls...
Ivories tickled and melodies twirled—
but sad tears dripped like crystal pearls.

A virtuoso on every stage...
the featured chanteuse of a golden age.
Her talent and tone was legendary...
her sickness so often incendiary.

Such paradox at every turn—
fame like a flame, she let it burn.
Two wicks on the candle at either end—
both burning brightly, the wax to spend.

A jazz life filled with contradictions—
so many highs, so many addictions.
All of the blues from a tortured soul—
so many lows, so little control.

Confined to asylums and padded cells...
nightmarish dreams and personal hell.
A blues no band would want to play—
the tragic night of Lady Day.

Beyond Category

To make a poet and paint him black...
to give him a musical basis of fact,
to dress him in top hat, vest and tails,
to place melody as the wind in his sails—
Here was a genius beyond rebuke.
Here was his eminence.
Here was the Duke.

So much music inside the man—
Fantasies in Black and Tan...
Satin Doll and Caravan...
Solitude and a Solid Old Man.

Lyrical wonder with every note—
Jazz Convulsions, silk topcoat...
The singular petal of music's rose,
the Bouncin' Buoyancy ever grows.
The Duke stepped out of the picture frame.
The musical canon was never the same.

So much rhythm inside his soul—
like Louis, and Ella, and Jelly Roll...
a Rhapsody, in part Creole...
A Blues Serenade that fills the bowl.

Conductor, leader of the band—
piano savant, at the Steinway Grand...
composer, arranger, so deft of hand...
jazz revelations, at his command.
We love to hear the maestro's story.
His genius we deem, beyond category.

So much novel improvisation—
cascades of complex syncopation...
the Snake Hip Dance, a mad gyration,
moving brown hips across the nation.

Jazz lovers, never you worry—
CD's abound with Sir Duke's glory...
a musical life's bold allegory.
His vision was clear, never blurry.
The verdict is in from the jury.
This Duke is beyond category.

427 Mass. Ave.

It's the legendary Wally's spot...
the dream of a brother named Joe Walcott...
the dream of a transplanted Bajan boy.
the first brother man to ever enjoy,
the status of owning it all.
In a place like Boston, imagine that—
a Black man standing tall.
Man, they called it the Paradise.
Man, the sounds were mighty nice.
Jazz lovers down for a chilled urban stroll—
with a sax man that oozes complete control,
or a drummer kickin' out blues and soul,
and a bass player lookin' to coax and cajole.
Jazz lovers came to spot built by Joe,
where music bathed in the after-glow...

The jammin' began in '47...
for what would become the Hub's jazz heaven...
joining the joints that became jazz legend,
the High Hat, the Wig Wam and Storyville—
where the big names always topped the bill...
The intersection of Mass. and Columbus—
hardly a real jazz fan among us,
hasn't flocked to the spot.
Asa Randolph and MLK,
dug Sassy Sarah and Lady Day.
One of the joints on the "Chitlin' Circuit",
brothers and sisters loved to work it.
Unwelcome at many spots down South,
they heard of Wally's by word of mouth.
Breakin' down the color line—
made for jazz that was super fine.

A different Mecca for Malcolm X,
an after-party for who was next...
The uptown whites came down from the Square,
to the spot where the flow was beyond compare.

When Joe left the scene, his kin took the reins,
Caribbean kin, with the juice in their veins.
They carry on the jazz tradition—
their "Pops" began as lifelong ambition.
Staging headliners for locals to savor,
they sprinkled in a new jack flavor.
Students anxious to hone their skills,
with top flight players, no hype, no frills.
From Berklee and the conservatories,
they jam in late-night laboratories.
A jazz incubator to college kid brains—
aspiring Ellas, Monks, and Coltranes.

No manic drama...
No tryin' to be cool...
No gourmet kitchen...
or shooting pool.
Nothing to move the music from first—
all kinds of potions to quench the thirst.
Not tryin' to be, somethin' they're not—
A four-star grill, or a disco spot.
Never an issue with color or race...
nobody judged by the hue of their face.
Black, brown and white in jazzy embrace...
all kinds of stories to tell 'bout the place.
Wally's Cafe, at 427...
the sound, still mighty fine...
Original spot was 428—
they moved in '79...

Live music played by the best in the land,
joined by young lions to spice up the band.
Live music played, all three-sixty-five—
keepin' the flame of Hub jazz alive.

Channeling Zora

Florida tried to stifle her sun.
In Harlem, her dreams would syrup and run.
Zora's eyes were watching God.
Zora's mind was wild and free.
Zora's heart was earth and sod.
Zora wrote her elegy.
Her feelings let her story flow.
Passion fueled her blazing glow.
They called her rebel and firebrand...
called her fierce, like Promethean man.
Who is this dazzling woman—
complex like warring souls?
Push-pull emotions surging,
like distant, magnetic poles.
Read between the pulsing lines...
twisted rhythms like ivy vines.
Feel the danger in unbridled spirit...
Ear to the ground and you might hear it.
This is no diva, no earthly actress.
This is the muse,
at war with her blackness.

Jazz Romance

They met at the corner,
of jazz and the blues.
He swung on the ones.
She swayed on the twos.

He could play the rhythm.
She could sing the rhyme.
There's was a love supreme,
metered in 3/4 time.

The band was tight.
The night was young.
Her eyes were as smoky—
as the air that hung...

Thick and sweet,
as the bass man's beat,
tight like the butt
on the drummer's seat.

She hit the high note—
with the sax and flute...
Like Billie and Ella,
she was jazz astute.

Meanwhile, he made
that guitar twang,
in tandem—
with every note she sang.

The house was hushed,
in grateful rapture,
with every emotion,
her song would capture.

Capturing longing—
capturing pain,
capturing the need,
to love again.

Jazz and romance in equal parts—
the passion flows as the music starts.
A brown bossa nova of glossy flair...
darting like fireflies, tumbling in air.

They met at the corner,
of jazz and the blues.
He swung on the ones.
She swayed on the twos.

Lena the Tigress

Tigress borne of sepia light...
deep in the heart of Brooklyn's sight.
Straddling the tight ropes of black and white,
a beautiful siren, angel of night.

A feisty redbone with smoky eyes...
a lilting vibrato, husky and wise.
She of the storied Stormy Weather,
solid as brass, but light as a feather.

Lena was magic on the silver screen.
Her beauty, electric in every scene.
Lena had passion for life and art.
Dancing and singing would set her apart.

They called her Bronze Venus...
no need to ask why—
For speaking between us,
that lady was fly.

Lena, a tigress of silken claws...
creamy skin that made men pause.
A mixture of cultures and plural race,
her beauty matched a fiery grace.

Embracing blackness as her own,
she sought to make each stage her home.
Yet often bigotry denied,
her forceful sense of racial pride.

The Cotton Club baby of Adelaide Hall—
A teen prodigy, her gifts would enthrall.
Later enamored with Duke and Stray'...
she sang with the greats for many a day.

Making her way to Hollywood —
the starlet life was not always good.
LA and Vegas and New York too,
mixed in her life as Black, white and blue.

Still her grander vision prevailed...
and a wonderful life in time was hailed.
Tony's and Grammy's would testify,
to more than a Cabin in the Sky.

The Lady and Her Music toured...
to huge acclaim and new love poured,
into the diva's grand profile...
attracted to her grace and style.

Lena, the tigress, wild and refined —
leaped beyond the color-line.
Striped like a bold, exotic fan,
a life perfected in black and tan.

Nikki Rosa Too

I read a Nikki Giovanni poem
today—
and there's something different
about the voice…
about the choice…
about the noise, and the splendor, and the blackness—
of the thorn among roses,
in literature's garden.
The passionate fires have cooled.
The frenzied tempos have slowed.
Today—
the gentleness
of womanly maturity
and Godly grace
have finally prevailed,
over the bluster of
youthful revolution
and inherited dissidence.

Marvin's Gone

I've got to say it,
"what's going on?"
The music's dying,
'cause Marvin's gone.

What's happenin' brother?
Who's to blame?
The soulful standard—
the singular name.

Luther gave us
a soulful feeling.
But nothing like Marvin's
sexual healing,

Those earthy duets
with Tammi Terrell—
they had a sound
you could always tell.

He left us sighing,
"Mercy me…"
as he sang to make
the spirit free.

Lyrics we still
must think upon…
the music's dying,
'cause Marvin's gone.

Naima

Coltrane had it exactly right—
A lilting tenor in the still of night...
many a note in each melody...
many a tune with true mastery.

And yet a special lyric persists,
the love of a maiden you barely kissed...
A song of the maiden's purity,
sweet on your reed like harmony.

A woman's scent you can't forget,
a hint of sadness each note regrets...
Naima's voice the still refrain...
Echoes her life, in joy and pain.

Melodic phrasing, in sheets of sound...
an equal in smoothness, as yet not found—
A gateway to the modern jazz nation,
peculiar chords and improvisation.

Coltrane changes, measured in thirds...
the kind of music that doesn't need words.
A love supreme in a smoke-filled club—
soothes the soul like a belly rub.

Slow and restrained, no pride or bluster—
Still lush and rich, shining with luster.
Orchestrated, romantic flow...
the master's mouth would magically blow.

Soon the entire pantheon plays...
every note that the master conveys.
Tyner and Walton and Pharaoh Sanders...
flatter his phrasing, no slights, or slander.

Playing Naima, your signature ballad...
each note embraced, each sentiment valid.
A standard of jazz known the world over—
in cities of glass and gardens of clover.

Lifting up jazz in Giant Steps...
from every sax man's book of reps.
Blue like Miles with a haunting lyric,
still the lovers flock to hear it.

—THE BEAUTIFUL FAITH—

"At the bottom of patience one finds heaven."

AFRICAN PROVERB

A Baby Boy All Draped in White...

A baby boy all draped in white...
the hope of the world on a moon-lit night.
The lambs in the manger are quietly bleating.
The angels and kings, their watch now completing.
The star in the East has beckoned them come—
to hear as the stable boy plays on his drum.
To witness the birth of a Savior and Lord,
and fall to their knees at this powerful Word.

The Word made flesh through a Virgin's womb...
the Truth and the Life in an outside room.
A Shepherd who'd someday survive the tomb,
and conquer death, returning soon.
The Word made flesh, I am that I am...
Immanuel, the Lord's true lamb.
Messiah, Teacher, the Holy One...
The Father's only Begotten Son.

All the earth once knew these things,
and kept in their hearts the light He brings.
This is the light we need even now...
beyond the masters, to which we may bow.
Not made for TV, a movie, or such—
we need this Jesus so very much.
It's not Youtube or a facebook page.
We're waging war in the Twitter age.

This is the truth of the Christmas story—
but we lose this truth in stress and worry.
We lose this truth in the enemy's lie,
of extravagant gifts piled up too high.
We lose this truth in his plan to deceive,
and make us think we're blessed to receive.
We lose this truth in an attitude,
that cancels what should be gratitude.

In a turbulent time and a perilous place—
a world full of danger He came to face.
The Advent of His matchless grace,
made slow the demon's advancing pace.
He came to set the captives free.
Even now, that's you...and that's me.
He came to establish His Father's plan
in the heart of every Godly man.

Now is that day, all bright and new—
the time for all, His plan to view.
Let us begin to witness and pray.
Let us give freely...yes give, everyday.
Come and regard this blessed event,
as a time to refresh, to forgive and repent.
Cast off the enemy's gold-plated lie.
Embrace now this gift, as the Savior draws nigh.

Don't wonder or fear the miraculous signs.
His mercy will cross political lines.
Creation will know of His sovereign might,
and pray for His favor by day and by night.
The door to salvation He opened for all,
in a Bethlehem stable, a donkey's stall.
Christ the King, you must remember...
and celebrate, here in December.

A baby boy all draped in white...
the hope of the world on a moon-lit night.
The lambs in the manger are quietly bleating.
The angels and kings, their watch now completing.
The star in the East has beckoned them come—
to hear as the stable boy plays on His drum.
The Lord of all Hosts came down from above...
to bathe a dark world in the light of His love.

Brown Skin and the Beautiful Faith

Brown skinned brothers,
I'm speaking in the flow.
The Lord has shone his light,
and I'm basking in the after-glow.
Stacks and stacks of rhymes
in my head,
'bout a savior who lives...
Oh no—
He's not dead.
So for all who will listen,
and all who will learn,
the lyrics will guide you
to live and not burn.
For the fire that comes
the next time consumes—
when the reign of the Son
in the earth resumes.
The beautiful faith
is his gift to us all—
delivered by Christ,
when we answer
His call.

Creation Waits

Science calls it evolution...
a cosmic slop of dissolution.
Yet every single, complex cell,
has a different tale to tell.

How could such a grand design,
by accident be so refined?
Each sunset and every star...
without a hand, be flung so far.

Without a hand of great direction,
how axon and dendrite connection—
adroitly moving muscle and bone...
rushing blood to every zone?

Every tissue, each complete—
nothing lacking, no conceit,
a marvelous, perfected feat...
existing at the Master's seat.

Creation waits expectantly,
the architect's resplendency...
in every mother's pregnant push—
in every forest, glade and bush.

Science touts the "big bang theory"—
makes the Godly man grow weary.
Ever the apologist,
he sees all that science missed.

The forming of each mountain span—
geology, without a plan?
Each ocean filled with vibrant life,
without a master surgeon's knife?

The rings of life in every tree—
mere chlorophyll and chemistry?

The wealth of apples in every seed,
without a planter's wondrous deed?

The spinning of the Potter's wheel,
is not a myth...and God is real.
To shape a man from warm, soft clay—
this is the Potter's passion play.

Creation waits, as the tale unfolds...
as we ponder the value
of silver and gold,
and diamonds emerge from stony holds.

Who could really add dispute—
Godly workings still refute?
Men of science, spirit feels...
Creation waits...
as God reveals.

I Heard Dude Say

I'm tryin' to tell you,
I heard dude say—
break out the stash son.
I'm here to pay.

It's Friday and I just got paid.
Let me get that platinum grade.
I know you got some killer chronic.
Pump that beat and let's get sonic.

This knot of mine is shrinkin' fast.
Gin and juice, we had a blast.
We closed the bar.
I bought four rounds.
Now we're huntin',
like drunk bloodhounds.

Comatose, blitzed, annihilated...
just a step ahead of the man.
I know I can't get violated...
back to the joint is not the plan.

Can't I hear the wee, small voice,
showin' me another choice?
Why has Satan's druggin' demon,
steady got a brother schemin'?

I steal.
I lie.
I don't know why.
But quittin'—
I won't even try.

This curse has got a hold of me.
Where's the love to set me free?

I'm tryin' to tell you—

I heard dude say…
Jesus—the truth,
the life, and the way.

I lost my family, my home, and my hope…
ain't got nothin' but anger and dope.
A brother is finding it hard to cope—
Maybe I'll try a gun or a rope.
But what did I hear?
What did dude say?
Jesus, the bread of life
shows the way.

Salvation assurance, eternally free.
Where do I go, this wonder to see?
Why would he want a wretch like me?
How can such a miracle be?

So I made my way to that church
on the hill…
Toting my demons
for Jesus to kill.
It won't be pretty.
Man, I'm a sight…
too filthy and gritty.
to save overnight.

I need to get clean and washed right away.
I need to be taught to fast and to pray.
I need to confess my sin and shame.
I've got to realize, this ain't no game.

Still, I'm oh so happy,
because I heard dude say—
he'll give your life new meaning
if you just accept Him today.

Elevation Theory

It's a theory for some, but the Prophet teaches
a gospel of love the disciple reaches.
The Savior has opened a heavenly door,
that lowers the ceiling and raises the floor.

Come to the city that sits on the hill,
where the saints sell out and the Son paid the bill.
Come light a candle and raise it up high,
acknowledge the master of earth, sea and sky.

What are you doing with the rest of your life?
Have you given in to the world's sin and strife?
My Father asks if you can relate
to His master plan to elevate.

Out of the shadows of sadness and shame—
a plan that lifts to a higher plane...
Out of the depths of your pain and hurt—
a plan that cleanses the enemy's dirt.

He's teaching mankind through a servant's voice,
to renew its strength with a higher choice.
He's teaching the Christian, the Muslim, the Jew—
His plan for me and His plan for you

Jesus the son is the liberator.
His blood, shed for all is the elevator,
that leads each lamb to this higher ground,
where the lost have now become the found.

It's a theory for some, but there's ample proof
that the Son is the Life, the Way and the Truth.
He is the Shepherd, the Bishop of Souls.
Realize through Him, your destiny's goals.

Scaling now each rung of the ladder...
going beyond the gossip and chatter

of haters, debunkers, and faith debaters,
achieving the worship to which our Christ caters.

See us rising—
hanging the banner of God without rival.
See us surging—
building the Church of the new saints revival.
See us climbing—
going beyond just basic survival.
See us leading—
making a path for the True Vine's arrival.

Not just talk, or philosophy,
but the word made flesh in all majesty...
The Bread of Life for the hungry soul,
the Light of the World for the young and the old.

If you must theorize—
this is elevation...
as the people of God,
move beyond deprivation—
as the faith of the saints
signals life activation.

If you must hypothesize—
this is levitation...
as Abraham's sons
rise beyond limitation—
as dominion authority
breeds soul captivation.

If you must rationalize—
this is impartation...
as the Father releases
a strong generation—
as the call on our lives
yields righteous relations.

It's a theory for some, but the Word is perfected
in the Living Water of the Son resurrected.

He is the Dayspring, the Bright Morning Star—
the Chief Cornerstone of a God beyond par.

His word has ordered our destiny,
defeating life's chaos entirely...
proclaiming the dance and a worshiper's way,
entreating His children to fast and to pray.

Praying through the flood of denial...
Praying though the thorns of the trial...
Praying though the sins that defile...
Praying beyond convention and style.

Proclaiming favor throughout the land...
Proclaiming the move of the Master's hand...
Proclaiming the gospel of love and of peace...
Proclaiming a time when all wars will cease.

Dancing for all the world to see...
Dancing into our shared legacy...
Dancing before a Risen King...
Dancing that soars on the eagle's wing.

A higher love we'll never see—
than the love of the Holy Trinity.
The Father, the Son, and the Spirit as one,
renewing all flesh in consecration

It's a theory for some, but our revelation
is Christ the King of emancipation—
filling our store and lifting our station,
raising our lives to a new elevation.

Lifting the kingdom community...
creating love and unity...
constructing sin immunity...
Almighty Holy Trinity.

The Father, the Son and the Spirit as one—
renewing all flesh in consecration.

The Race I Run Today

This race I run is not my own.
The Father put me on a path.
He said, "this is the way, walk ye in it."
So I laced up my boots
and I started to move.

I moved to the right
and I saw life and light,
and the love of my children.

I moved to the left
and I saw joy and jazz,
and the jubilee of His promise—
for all who know Him,
who are called to His purpose,
obeying His perfect will.

I climbed up the hill and I saw elevation.
I fell down the hill and I learned determination.
I fell down...but I got up.

I climbed up the stairs and rested on the landing.
The road below is so demanding.
I fell down...but I got up.

I climbed up the ladder, struggling to make it.
Sometimes I even had to fake it.
I fell down...but I got up.

In darkest night, He lifted me.
Beyond my sight, He lifted me.
With all His might, He lifted me.
I fell down...but I got up.

He showed me the peace that reconciles.
He showed me the joy that always smiles.
He shouldered my burden all the while.
I fell down...but I got up.

I waded into the shallow stream
and found the living waters.

I knelt in the muddy brook
and felt the earth between my toes.
I dived into the deep end of the ocean
and learned the truth of my heart's longing.

I long for the laughter of my daughters.
I long for the strength of my sons.
I long for the wee small voice that answers my prayers
and assuages my sadness—
with the miracle of His healing,
and the wisdom of His counsel.

I long for the witness of His might.
I long for his comfort, late at night.
I long to be marvelous in His sight.

My Father put me on a path.
He said—
"This is the Way, the Truth, and the Life."

I opened the door,
and walked into my destiny,
finding all the best of me—
in the faces of my progeny.

I opened the door
and I ran into my history,
uncovering the mystery—
of a black and brown-skinned legacy.

I opened the door
and I made this strong connection—
to the hedge of His protection
and my own complete reflection...

A reflection of His perfect face...
A reflection of his matchless grace...
A reflection of this precious race...

The race I run today.

Dedicated to Barbara Wright,
On the occasion of her occasion of he 70ᵗʰ birthday
November 23, 2012

May I Serve You?

I'm called to this place
and so are you—
to bless the Kingdom
as servants do.

We are the faces.
We are the hands—
who live for His grace
and honor His plans.

We greet you warmly
on Sunday morn.
We move the cone,
when you toot your horn.

We show your family
to empty seats.
Every Sunday,
our service repeats.

We set the tables.
We straighten the chairs.
We clean the carpets—
and vacuum the stairs

We set the stage
for sight and sound—
the altar raised
as holy ground.

We meet you early
for morning prayer.
We drive the vans
that get you there.

We are the shepherds,
that round up the sheep.
We're wide awake,
when others sleep.

This is the day
that the Lord has made.
We bring the troubled,
comfort and aid.

We are the soldiers,
who stand at each post.
We serve the Bishop
tea and wheat toast.

We watch the babies,
while pastor preaches.
We are the nursemaids
and Sunday school teachers.

We are the Pastor's
Men in Black.
Don't get it twisted,
we got His back.

We serve the wafers.
We serve the wine.
We pass the trays,
so you may dine.

We shout Hosanna
in praise of our King—
inviting you all,
to join as we sing.

We even write
the words on the screen—
to keep the worship
honest and clean.

We dance like David—
in spirit and truth.
We are true servants,
like Esther and Ruth.

We will take up
your offering.
Remember, the tithe—
belongs to the king.

We move the youth
toward revolution—
embracing faith
as the final solution.

We hug you tight,
in loving service...
trusting our hugs
won't make you nervous.

We offer our gifts
in sacrifice—
hoping your "tweets"
will mostly be nice.

We serve the king,
as faith commands.
We serve with our hearts,
our souls, and our hands

This is the way
the savior leads.
We've all been called,
as the kingdom needs.

Now it's your turn
to leave the boat.
You can't complain,
if you never vote.

We love your thanks
and accolades—
but hope you all
will sharpen your blades.

Put on you armor.
Take up your post.
Present your gifts
to the Lord of Hosts.

May I serve you?
A Godly question...
Answering yes,
is the right suggestion.

You'll plant a seed
in a kingdom row...
becoming the water,
that makes faith grow.

You'll be the salt,
that seasons the meal...
served by disciples,
who heard Christ's appeal.

And then He'll say,
"Good servant well done.
You are my daughter.
You are my son."

What Do Men Call Me?

What do men call me?
Do they proclaim,
the glory of my wondrous name?
What do men call me?
Do they see in me,
the redeeming light of eternity?
What do men call me?
Can they not tell,
I am Beloved Immanuel.

Jehovah Nissi—
I am the banner,
faith revealed in triumphant manner.
Jehoveh Jireh—
I provide,
the territory expanded wide.
Jehovah Rapha—
I heal the land,
all sickness falls as I wave my hand.
Jehovah Shalom—
the prince of peace,
at my command, all wars must cease.

I am the Father's bread of life.
My body and blood are a sacrifice...
the only stream from which may flow,
the living water that makes faith grow.

I am the Son...The King of Kings...
the Lord of whom the psalmist sings.
I came that men would be set free.
I came to restore God's family.

Immaculate birth in a virgin womb—
I came to conquer death and the tomb.
I am the prophet.
I am the priest.
I came to serve the covenant feast.

Beyond any lie or satanic deed,
by potentates of demonic seed...
Beyond the gauntlet,
beyond the sword,
beyond the flight
of the falconer's bird...
beyond the report of
sin and strife—
I am the groom.
This church is my wife.

Beyond a library full of the stories,
of earthly kings and their heathen glories—
beyond empire,
beyond dragon fire,
beyond knights and knaves
and the men they call sire,
I am the faithful witness of hosts—
destroying the enemy's monsters and ghosts.

Does history seek to intervene—
remove the gospel from this scene,
the bridegroom leave without a queen?

Do scholars seek to relegate—
my walk on earth to understate,
my miracles to violate?

Does science seek to recreate—
the bread of life reformulate,
the lamb of God reanimate?

Do men raise idols before my door—
abandon the sick,
and curse the poor?

I gaze into my Father's face—
expanding the boundaries of time and space,
increasing the store of each soul He touches,
beyond the pain of sin's vile clutches.

Beyond the stream,
so clear and still...

Beyond the dreams,
that sorrows kill.

Beyond sight, sound
and other senses...
Beyond all barriers,
borders and fences.

Beyond the specter of
disbelief..
Beyond the despoiler,
the ghost and the thief.

What do men call me,
this bright shining day?
Do they call me the truth,
the life and the way?

I dwell above
the reach of the seasons,
the logic of reason,
the vastness of time and
the might of ten legions.

I dwell beyond
the bars of steel cages,
the devil's foul wages,
and all of the ink
on a poet's pages.

I dwell within
the Father's true heart.
Wielding His staff,
I make oceans part.
Wielding His rod,
I summon His wrath.
Bearing His standard,
I show men His path.

In this place of worldly things —
Do men not reckon
the King of Kings?
Do men not pray to

the Son of Man?
Do men not fathom
His master Plan?

This is the day that
the Lord has made.
Mine is the scepter,
the ring and the blade.

I'm key to the lock
of every man's fate.
I'm key to the lock
at Eden's gate.

I am the Shepherd—
the Master's right hand,
repairing the breach,
restoring the land.

I am the King of both Gentile and Jew.
I am the Savior, Faithful and True.
Teacher, Judge, the Holy One...
The Father's only begotten son.
Prophet, Messiah...I'm these things too.
Beloved servant—
from Him,
for you.

When all men bow to worship me,
all the world will be set free.
When all men lift their hands in praise,
I will extend the length of their days.
I am the Prince of my Father's peace.
I came that war and hate would cease.

When the enemy seeks to steal my throne—
remember me as the cornerstone.
When the world suggests another thing—
be not afraid to call me King.
My kingdom reigns this very day.
I am the truth, the life, and the way.

A Whole Number

I'm going to love myself today.
It's not a resolution,
or a revolution…
It's just my contribution—
to this coupled up community.

It's just me, myself, and I.
But I don't need an alibi,
for being by myself.

It was not easy
to get to this place.
The mirror reflected
a real ugly face,
and a shadow
that wasn't mine alone.

I made my own bed.
But not content to sleep alone,
I've stuff for which I must atone.
Regret has been my pillow—
and my dreams have been disturbed.

But I've come through
the fire and the flood,
mixed with
the mire and the mud…
Now I'm saved by
the Savior and His blood.

I've been through
the chaos and the din,
of past attractions
to lust and sin…
Now I've made myself
only His to win.

I have learned to appreciate
my own company...
and all the good things,
that the Father made me.

I'm good and satisfied,
with the God who dwells inside.
It's not a platitude...
It's an attitude...
In fact,
I'm filled with gratitude...
for gifts of the heart,
and fruit of the spirit.

My numerical progression—
by my own sincere confession,
is no theory of regression,
I'm a number, whole and prime,
not a tangent or cosine.

So please don't trip at all,
when I show up at the ball
without a date,
a partner, or a mate.

It's all good.

The one He has for me
is single, whole and free,
maturing in Godly destiny...
and waiting in the wings.
Waiting for the agreement.
Waiting for the respect.
Waiting for the covenant of faith,
that leads to the vows of trust
and the ties that bind.

Until then...
my love and true romance,
my partner at the dance,
my soulmate and my chance,
is clear.

I love the God in me...
the Jesus who sets me free.
One who exists in three—
allowing me just to be,
just the one I am.

And one is a whole number too.

—HOME SLICE—

"Do not throw away the oars before the
boat reaches the shore."

CONGOLESE PROVERB

Chicken Sunday

Snap, crackle, pop
in a cast iron pan...
secret seasonings
and man oh man.
Momma's makin'
my favorite meal.
It's Chicken Sunday
and here's the deal—
breasts and thighs...
and legs and wings
Hush—
I ain't talkin' 'bout
sexual things.
Better get your mind
up out the gutter...
Have some respect.
I'm talkin' 'bout mother.

There in the kitchen,
romancin' the stove—
with Old Bay, Adobo
cumin and clove.
Potato salad
is in the fridge coolin'...
Gonna' get my grub on
and that's no foolin'.
Momma's makin'
my favorite meal.
It's Sunday son,
and that's for real.

Can't you smell
the cornbread bakin'—
and Nana's collard greens,
Auntie Zonie's N'awlins dirty rice,
and Zenie's butter beans...
Seven-up cake

and pecan pie..
food so good,
make a grown man cry.

It's something that
don't happen on Monday.
So Hallelujah—
for Chicken Sunday.

Dedicated to our moms, Jean and Roberta...
"A mother's love is food for the spirit and the soul."
August 2011

Elena's Song

Wasn't because I didn't have game,
didn't want challenge—
and couldn't stand fame.

I'm a simple girl and don't need much,
just family and friends—
just Lizzie and such.

I know I bailed on the folks in Storrs,
never walked on the court—
never walked through the doors.

But they went on without me—
won championships,
despite the whispers of idle lips.

I wasn't a flake, or disloyal a bit.
In fact being loyal,
was a big part of it.

I had to go home and couldn't have stayed—
couldn't care less that,
I never had played.

Left the bright lights and the national scene.
Went home to the love,
where the grass was most green.

When they sing my song as I hope they might—
just let it be said that,
I kept home in sight.

For Elena Delle Donne,
with respect and admiration...
March 29, 2013

Our Girls

Our girls speak in proper pedantic tones.
Our girls write letters on laptops and phones.
Our girls refuse to stop at the ceiling.
Our girls discover what faith is revealing.
Our girls sip soup without slurping sounds.
Our girls plant flowers all over the grounds.
Our girls can act and sing and dance.
Our girls are good at wearing the pants.
Our girls aren't scared or intimidated.
Our girls have egos that won't be deflated.
Our girls can dribble and pass and shoot.
Our girls can wear a mean power suit.
Our girls get in to all the best schools.
Our girls won't suffer ignorant fools.
Our girls have swag and high self-esteem.
Our girls live out the American dream.
Our girls read Morrison, Dickens and Joyce.
Our girls develop their own unique voice.
Our girls move mountains that get in their way.
Our girls can stand up and have their say.
Our girls aren't perfect; they make mistakes.
Our girls aren't phonies, posers, or fakes.
Our girls don't miss a school with no boys.
Our girls know how to put aside toys.
Our girls will follow their heart's desires.
Our girls will someday build global empires.
Our girls refuse to stop at the ceiling.
Our girls bust through it, once more
with feeling!

Dedicated to Maya Naomi Carter
and the class of 2012...
Woodward School for Girls, Quincy, MA

115

I'm the Daddy!

I ain't playin' with y'all.
If I told you once, I told you a thousand times...
Don't make me take off this belt.
Y'all gonna make me lose my mind, up in here.
For the last doggone time—
Who you think you talkin' to?
Oh, you must be high...
Do I have "stupid" written 'cross my forehead?
I'm tired of y'alls foolishness.
I want to see some butts, and I want to see 'em now!
You need Jesus.
Lord, please don't let me kill this boy!
Are you deaf?
I ain't your mother!
Child, you best get out my face!
What is your malfunction?
Keep it up, you hear—
Boy, I will knock you out!
Your butt better be home 'fore the streetlights come on.
Who you rollin' your eyes at?
If mama ain't happy, ain't nobody happy.
Oh, so you a grown man now?
Better get that bass out your voice.
Child, I'm 'bout to smack the taste out your mouth.
Don't let your mouth write no checks your behind can't cash.
'Cause I said so, that's why!
And you best not embarrass me and your mama up in here.
What part of "no" don't you understand?
Your problem is you got too much mouth!
My house, my rules...
As long as you live under my roof...
I didn't ask you for your opinion!
Keep your hands to yourself.
Don't start no mess, won't be no mess.
If Pookie and 'dem jump off a bridge, you gon' jump too?
Get your mind out the gutter.
Clean up that mess.

I brought you into this world, and I'll take you out.
You better act like you know.
I'm 'a wear that behind out!
Me and your mama raised you better'n this.
Don't say another word!
I'm about two seconds from losin' my reason.
I'm a beat you like you stole somethin'.
The maid died.
'Cause I'm the Daddy!
You wanna act like a witch, go cut me a switch.
Better clean that plate.
Keep cuttin' them eyes, you hear?
What you talkin' 'bout, "hand me downs".
It was good enough for your sister, and it's good enough for you.
My mama didn't raise no fool.
My money paid for that.
Get a job—sha na na na, sha na na na na…
I'll wash that mouth out wit' soap.

Now I don't want to steal any classic lines…
Just stop me and say, "Hey that one's mine!"

Everyone's parents' use to say,
something like this…
in their own special way

I'm here to remind you and make it clear—
we need "tough love" in the atmosphere.

So if you're reliving that terrible time…
remember the reason, he beat your behind.

We spare the rod and spoil the child,
only to watch them go buck wild.

Yet the Bible warns us not to neglect—
teaching obedience, faith and respect.

We shouldn't send them out in the world,
without the banner of love unfurled.

If we want the Father to lengthen their days,
we have to show them His word and His ways

I'm here to remind you and make it clear—
Agape love is spoken here.

But just in case you didn't know...
I'm the Daddy and I said so!

In the Kitchen

It's black and white.
I'm wrong; you're right.
The truth is I
don't want to fight.
If you want it dark,
I'll shut off the light...
and try to be humble
with all of my might.

My boys might say
you're nagging me.
That's not the truth
that sets us free.
I'll let them know
it isn't cool,
to think you take me
for a fool.

It's black and white.
I'm wrong; you're right.
I shouldn't have said,
"go fly a kite."
We'll compromise
on all your wishes.
Yes, my darling,
I'll do the dishes.

The Bible says
you are my gift.
So seeking to
repair this rift—
foul spirits
I must try to lift.
'Cause clearly
you are more than miffed.

I am your husband.
You are my wife.
That look, ooh Lordy—
cuts like a knife.
It's black and white.
I'm wrong; you're right.
Can't we just
have peace tonight?

Ode To The Ville (Act Like You Know...)

It's about those streets
where we laughed and played.
It's about that church
where our family prayed.
It's about that school
where we learned it all.
And about that park
where we played some ball.

Every adult knew every child,
and would light them up—
for actin' wild.
Didn't take no disrespect...
seldom did you see neglect.
DSS didn't come 'a calling...
no time-outs, no pit bull maulings.

The Ville, where life
was a true inkwell.
Every clan had tales to tell.
Doc' Kountze kept the history.
Of Medford's chocolate mystery.
Riding his bike with papers and files...
Telling our stories, across the miles.

Simple pleasures,
too many to mention.
Though here's a few
for your attention...
Penny candy at the Little Store,
pickles and hot dogs and so much more.
Building models and cooking classes
at the Center, where many a good day passes.
The soda fountain at Kale's Drug Shoppe
A bay of Cain's, and an ice cold pop.

Simple pleasures,
too many to mention.
A pound of cure
and an ounce of prevention.
Not to say we didn't suffer.
Even love's not a perfect buffer.
Many left the scene for good.
But never left the neighborhood.

Remember little Charlie Tanner?
Withered away in a tragic manner.
Remember Fruitman, Frank French folks
Remember Puddin', Smitty had jokes.
Remember Mike Heywood, funnier still.
Suicide's such a bitter pill.
Remember Dana, lost and forlorn?
and Nelly, from the village torn?
Youngbloods meltin' away from the scene.
Sometimes the Ville could be just a bit mean.

Still the loss of a brother
was never the point...
The strength of our families
made this place the joint.
Allowed us to mourn
as together we stood,
without departing the neighborhood.
You can take the homeboy out of the Ville,
but the voice of his hometown
remains in his will.

Tom Wolfe said that you couldn't go home.
I'm disputing that claim in this little poem.

Simple pleasures,
too many to mention.
Retired well
on a gov'ment pension.
Parents would raise
their kid's kids too.

In homes they owned,
through banks they knew.

Sunday sermons with OGP—
home at Shiloh, so peaceably.
West Medford Baptist, two blocks away.
We knew that this was the Father's day.

After church, young folk, all migratin'—
to kung fu flicks and roller skatin'.
The Paramount and the Bal-a-Roue…
I'd be hangin…what about you?

Regulators kept it frosty—
mess with the Ville and it could be costly.
Wolf and Whit and Eddie Lockett,
kept some beat-down in their pocket.

Afro-American Society—
at Medford High, made us feel free.
Ebonettes had jackets too…
serious sisters, a no-joke crew.

Loved that home in the Mystic Valley.
For Lincoln Street, just cut through the alley,
off of Jerome, by Humpty's shop.
Leave the sides, just a bit off the top.

My Baby Girl and I

Dear sweet child,
I'm your biggest fan—
though we don't see eye to eye.
I'm hoping to make the best of things.
Lord knows I really try.
Still we miscommunicate,
my baby girl and I.

She's filling out quite well,
in all the righteous places.
And daddy's gettin' real nervous,
'cause of dudes with smiling faces.
Yo homes, don't get it twisted, thinkin' she's so fly.
She's just a kid and I'm the man.
It's baby girl and I.

She wants to hang and party down—
painting her face with green and brown,
drive the Benz and park in town...
turns my smile into a frown.
I ask her, "Are you high?"
My baby girl and I.

Still I know, the day will come—
when I must be relenting.
And so this little piece I write,
is just a father venting.
I cannot lock her in her room,
although I wonder, "Why?"

Oh never let it cease to be,
my Baby Girl and I.

Red Velvet Cake

Back in the day…
in the sleepy south—
the maids baked somethin'
to water your mouth.

The flavor was real,
though the color looked fake.
Them sisters concocted
a red velvet cake.

Classically layered,
with mild chocolate flavor…
red velvet cake is
something to savor.

Richly adorned
with sweet butter cream,
that smooth silky frosting
between each seam.

The origin is hard to find.
Though legends of the urban kind,
persist up to this very day…
as recipes are put in play.

Still, if your path
is Brooklyn-bound—
at Cakeman Raven's
the best is found.

Some might argue,
and that's all right…
'cause Raven's cake
is out of sight.

Richly adorned
with sweet butter cream,
a white satin treasure
between each seam.

Dense and delicious,
with every bite...
I believe I will have
a slice tonight.

Sister Act

They go to her bedroom
most every night,
for the mother and daughter
pillow fight.

Too much fun
is being had —
tho' just for mum,
and not for dad.

He can't be party,
to such drama.
He's forced to leave it
to her mama.

They've gone beyond
the natural fact.
It's now become
a sister act.

He can't be privy
to secret glances,
or the quiet glee
of young romances.

Such catty gossip
and dishy tales —
His logic and
his patience fails.

He has no frame
of reference.
To mom he yields,
in deference.

They've gone beyond
the natural fact.
It's now become
a sister act.

They team up on him,
now and then—
two on one,
his will to bend.

Oh Daddy,
won't you take us please?
Don't make us get
down on our knees.

He loves them both
in different ways…
in different moments,
on different days.

They've gone beyond
the natural fact.
It's now become
a sister act.

To dad it seems
a bit bizarre—
that he must love them,
from afar.

Though true enough—
he spends the dime,
to waltz his loves
in three-four time.

Yet still he envies,
their moments like this…
the joy of a mother's
compassionate kiss.

They've gone beyond
the natural fact.
It's now become
a sister act.

—KIND OF BLUE—

"When an old man dies, a library burns to the ground."

CONGOLESE PROVERB

Elegy for Katrina's Wake

Many still cannot go home.
N'awlins listen to my poem.
Creole heart with a Cajun soul,
shrimp and grits, hot in a bowl.

Flooding waves and wind-torn days,
miracles sung by voices of praise...
The levees broke, the spirit held—
Tenth Parish blues as water swelled.

Katrina's wake lapped up their dreams—
lives under lakes and swollen moonbeams.
The second line, it marches on.
The poor folks sing a mournful song.

Soon beads and masks in Mardi Gras streets
and Black magic floating on Beausoleil beats,
and Shrimp Po'boys on soft baguettes...
brought N'awlins back for the tourist set.

Revelry peaks on reclaimed roads,
while nearby misery daily reloads.
Many now will never go home.
Cajun hearts still doomed to roam.

Where lies the soul of Creole rebirth-
Tenth Ward blues, no laughter or mirth-
A violent storm's turbulence shook the plain—
cov'ring race scars in mud and rain.

Many damp nights in the Superdome...
it's hot and rank and nothing like home.
Decent folk wallow in filth and squalor,
Where is the sheen of American valor?

Can you hear the trumpet man...
second line tears in a sorrow-song band.
Sour notes played in an uneven score,
no magic for the homeless poor.

Katrina's wake was color-struck—
Black folks mired in mold and muck.
Uptown types have fared much better.
The levees broke and the broke got wetter.

The levees broke into lowland blues,
of a cultural divide that was never news.
Shock and sadness, the after-math...
dirty waters and a shameful bath.

Soiling the plumes of the alouette...
the gentle skylark's poignant regret.
Many saints will never go home.
N'awlins hear my mournful poem.

Fragment for Trayvon, DJ, Sandy Hook and Jordan

Children should be the wealth of our community
like green grocers, great cobblers, and
faithful pastors,
their spirits buoyed with a notion of belonging.
They are the greatest gift we have to present
to a world of cynics, haters, and unbelievers.
Yet, the godless among us,
building walls of distrust—
navigate the sea of discontent
and open the doors for dark witness.

Children should be making funny faces,
like CGI avatars of Power Puff Girls and
Rice Crispy guys,
their eyes aglow with animated possibilities...
They should not be the hapless victims
of ages-old misconceptions of race, class, and human worth.
Pity the unhearing ears we too soon fill with ashes and dust—
forever removed from the laughter
that accompanies youthful exuberance,
young love, and nascent hope.

Children should be safe in certain places—
like strip malls, study halls and toilet stalls...
Let us only hear their voices—
their happy voices raised in raucous banter.
They should not be the panicked targets
of a gun-crazed misanthrope's denial of home and hopefulness—
bolting in bloody chaos before the maelstrom,
forever stripped of innocence or worse...
trapped, targeted and taken out...
young lives denied the promise of their path.

Children should be able to walk the air...
like Peter, once called to leave the boat,
buoyed by the faith of our fathers and
clothed in all the colors of a nation unbound.

They should not be statistical anomalies,
highlighting the lack of compassion in a system
that celebrates its freedom to stockpile arms,
holster peace, and shoot to kill…
harboring still a menacing penchant
for destroying its dark water pearls.

Dismissal

His bags were packed and neatly stacked
beside the parlor door.
She said in no uncertain terms—
he wasn't welcome anymore.

In doing all he knew to do,
he tried to reconcile.
He figured he could ride it out,
and come back in a while.

But the tone in her voice this time—
so permanent and strange.
The bitterness had multiplied
its hold like creeping mange.

The days of angry words,
and nights of silent rage—
had placed their flaming pledge of love
in an airless crystal cage.

He found a room at the "Y"—
and tried to settle in.
He sent his paycheck home...
and prayed a reprieve,
he'd shortly win.

But the tone in her voice this time—
haunted his every thought.
Like a stinging fly it dug in deep
to skin, stretched pink and taut.

She wouldn't respond to his texts or calls,
though he'd see her at church and shopping malls.
Her family shunned his presence too,
despite the loving things he'd do.

The pure and simple fact—
was that he'd been dismissed.
The valediction came,
without a loving kiss.

Indeed cruel circumstance,
had moved him to the gate.
Her steel resolve had blended
with the fury of her hate.

He wouldn't stoop to stalking—
For pride he couldn't beg.
The time had passed for talking.
There would be no reneg.

The loving bond they'd shared,
was surely at its end.
No fragments yet remained
for time and space to mend.
His honor mixed with sadness,
sped him to desperation.
Misery's thorny arms,
embraced him with resignation.

And soon, he'd cried out every anguished tear.
And soon, he'd suffered every nagging fear.
And soon, his bleeding heart would burn and sear.

He packed his bags in silence—
and squared away his room.
He trimmed his beard intently.
His hair he neatly groomed.

He wrote a note and signed it,
so friends would understand.
And then he stood and calmly took
the pistol in his hand.
He said a prayer of penitence,
and asked God to forgive.
He said the life he had right now,
he couldn't bear to live.

He wasn't one for long goodbyes,
and so—
He pulled the trigger once...
and let the life
he once knew go.

A sad valediction
without a kiss—
gone too soon,
he'd been dismissed.
His dying moments
were spent in despair—
a good man's climb,
up a perilous stair.
He never got to
his bucket list.
Gone to soon...
he'd been dismissed.

Dead Drunk

You're tolerance wasn't satisfied.
One taste just wouldn't gratify.
Man, you just kept on drinking.
Dude, what could you be thinking.

The night was young,
and the booze was flowing.
The jazz band swung,
and your buzz was growing.

Barkeep thought he knew you pretty well.
Hey, as far as he could really tell,
wasn't no thing with you and liquor—
He didn't feel the need to bicker.

Poured that whiskey, shot by shot...
Jack, Black Label, straight and neat.
Hour by hour, quite a lot...
dude, you never left the seat.

What silent rage were you trying to pacify?
What wrong were you seeking to rectify?
What sin were you trying to sanctify?
What pain were you trying to purify?
Kneeling at the altar of the last call—
what could be bettered with so much alcohol?

Barkeep knew you paid your tab...
should have thought to call a cab.
Instead he watched you stagger out the door,
barely standing up you downed one more.

You made it to your car with crooked gait.
Then you had a taste to get you straight...
from a hip flask in your pocket—
Then the key went in the socket.

The engine revved, the car lurched from its space.
Bleary-eyed, you couldn't gauge your pace.
The light was red you didn't stop.
The minivan felt the hammer drop.

Airbags deployed, and you never suspected—
that the minivan was so unprotected.
Two victims thrown 'bout fifty feet,
while you barely moved from your drunken seat.

What senseless folly had you wrought?
So many shots of Jack you bought...
What howling demon have you got?
How could you leave that tragic spot?

Suspended license, twice you're busted—
DUI and not to be trusted.
We're shocked to see another instance when,
you drink, and drink, and drink, then drive again.

Only, this time the victims perished and fell.
Now you're caught in a living hell.
Double vehicular homicide—
a mother and her daughter died.

Stolen from their family...
you created this tragedy.
A nightmare predicted at shot number one...
you used that car like a loaded gun.

Dead-drunk and now incarcerated...
reliving each day, the mess you created.
No one survived that awful ordeal.
Some scars, society just can't heal.

You're sober now, regretting that sight—
but the tremors come, in the dead of night.
Dead-drunk and driving, stupid and blind...
demons you'll never leave behind.

Ma Petite Îsle de Tragédie

Beloved home of blood and sand
Port of spices, rum, and stolen African flesh...
Pourquoi, c'est toujour la même chose.
Ma petite îsle de tragédie.

They flee from you for fortunes far away,
leaving travail in a tearful wake.
Ceux qui rient le vendredi, pleurent le dimanche.
(Those who laugh on Friday, will cry on Sunday.)
Ma petite îsle de tragédie.

Beyond warriors slain, potentates, pretenders and princes,
your promise yet remains in dreams.
Quelle heure est il? Quelle heure est il?
(What time is it? What time is it?)
Ma petite îsle de tragédie.

Has the God we love forsaken us?
Has he too fled with the fruit of our genius?
Plus ça change, plus c'est pareil.
(The more things change, the more they stay the same.)
Ma petite îsle de tragédie.

Now is the hour of our most urgent need.
Now is the day of our greatest reckoning.
Now is the truth of the Lord's power and grace in our lives.
Malheur à qui mal y pense.
(Woe to those who think evil.)

Amid the destruction of earthen upheaval —
amid the loss, the hunger, the desolation,
humble people cry out for a proud nation.
Mon Dieux, mes frères, mes pères...
Répondez s'il vous plaît!
Il faut souffrir pour être belle.
(To have beauty, suffering must be endured.)

Adieu à chacun pour soi.
(Farewell to every man for himself.)
Adieu ma petite île de tragédie.
Vive l'unité des Haitiens!
Vive le coup de maître!
Vive ma grande île des miracles.
Vive La République!

Who Hurt You My Child?

Who crept to your bed,
        in the dead of night?
And vowed in a whisper—
        this touch was right.
What uncle Sid, or cousin Sal,
        conspired to make you
his secret pal?

How desperate for
        your nubile flesh...
what wounds would cut you,
        deep and fresh?
Who coaxed, bribed
and beguiled?
Who hurt you
        my child?

Who plied your thoughts
        with promised treats...
then ravaged you
        beneath dark sheets?
What monstrous demons—
        love rejected,
found you lost,
        and unprotected?

What suicidal blanket covers—
        your wish to love,
and trust in others?
        Lost in the slumber
of absent mothers...
        scarred by the lust
of sinful brothers,
        who hunted in the night?

Who threatened you,
        with certain death…
for uttering
        a fearful breath?
Who made the peaceful
        kingdom wild?
Who hurt you
        my child?

What stain attacked,
        so forcibly—
and bound you up,
        sadistically?
What manner of abuse,
        or worse…
has victimized you,
        with this curse?

Who chased the light,
        from infant eyes…
bruised your arms,
        your chest, your thighs?
What beast of dark
intention crept—
into your silence,
        as you slept?

What pestilence—
        of humankind,
assaults with such
        a cruel design?
What could be
        much more reviled?
Who hurt you,
        my dear child?

What scourge in
        family relations,
now brings forth
these aberrations?

Mustn't our society
      kill this vile depravity?
Why instead this prosecution,
      as the late and last solution?
Where is this case
      of child rape filed?
How high are
      the cases piled?
How many innocents,
      defiled?
Who hurt you,
      my child?

Who that a God
of peace forgives—
yet in this state
of lust still lives?
Was not this sinful nature,
reconciled?
Good Lord...
who let him hurt you,
my dear child?

This Fire In My Chest

I don't know what they're talkin' bout.
But, something is turnin' me inside out.
Don't you hear my heartbeat pound?
I can't believe what these doctors found.
this fire in my chest...
They say it's cancer of the breast.
The signs are there and the blood
don't lie...
It stings the soul like a great gadfly.

Come on man, I'm not the one.
What other scans can you doctors run?
I don't have man-boobs; my stuff is tight.
I treat my body kind of right...
But the biopsies and other tests
reveal some ugliness in my chest.
So I'm flippin' cause I'm new to this.
And I'm trippin' on the clues I missed.

Now, we brothers bond over certain things,
Cars and hoops and buffalo wings.
Will my homeboys have some empathy,
for this lump they found inside of me?
It's not in the spot my boys would expect—
the spot that we always learned to protect.
More than likely they won't relate.
It's not my colon or my prostate.
Why would I get a mammogram,
as part of my yearly health exam?
No lead, asbestos or nicotine—
it's not my lungs; they're perfectly clean.
I'm only forty and kind of cut—
not quite a six-pack,
with a real nice butt.

Still—
there's fire raging in my chest.
They hush when they whisper
cancer and breast.

Let's look at the science, the numbers, the stats—
on malignant cells in tissues and fats.
It's one percent of the population,
a thousand per year in a cancer-prone nation.
Women afflicted one hundred times more,
by a killer that meets them at every door.

But the sisters…
umph, they got it on together.

They got 10K walks and 5K runs,
pretty pink ribbons and dozens of funds.
We men are lacking in education,
TV ads and a big foundation.
It's something we'd only snicker about,
not a cause to make us march and shout.
And the language is like some secret code…
Which are the ducts and what are the nodes?
Listen to this laundry list…
Who can fathom any of this?

Chronic Obesity—
Genetic abnormality –
Hyperestrogenism—
Klinefelter's syndrome—
Finasteride use—
Cirrhosis and Liver disease—
Negro please…
You never heard 'bout
most of these.

But the symptoms are there and easily seen—
if my eyes are open and my mind is keen.
Skin raw and puckered all over my pecs…
marauding cells that an x-ray detects…
sore red nipples, turning inside out…
muscle and nerve pain that make you shout…
constant tingling in the feet and hands—
can't be part of the Master's plan.

The language may be like a code…
but the revelation would soon explode—
and burn the flesh,

and bake the breast…
becoming, this fire in my chest.

Think it not perverse or strange,
like a hairless dog with a case of mange.
Cells mutate and rearrange.
Body parts forever change—
becoming, this fire in my chest.

The lesson is clear, the danger profound,
a silent killer with a deafening sound.
Thought it couldn't happen to me,
a woman's concern most definitely—
becoming, this fire in my chest.

Brothers we can't be
foot draggers…
hatin' on some
finger-waggers.
This enemy stuns.
The body staggers.
The will retreats.
The cycle repeats.

Embarassing, yes,
and surely rare…
but homeboys, we—
we must go there.
This defect can
infect us too.
It's happening to me.
It could happen to you.

I now believe.
They didn't lie—
no excuse,
no alibi.
I've got cancer of the breast…
this fire in my chest.

For my sister, friend and fellow poet, Chevonceil Echols…
Thank you for "Silent No More".
May, 2011

146

My Body's Not My Own

I walked those streets in certain pain.
Provocateur, purple fishnets and thong panties,
too much make-up and too little pride...
pimped out by a smooth-talking
social pariah.

Still a school girl —
could have been in bobby sox
and a poodle skirt...
A cheerleader and a bit of a flirt,
but nothing like this.

I walked those streets, a soul conflicted.
Star-crossed, stiletto heels and stony heart —
object of derision and desire,
never pursued by love,
just lust for hire.

Yes, a mama's pearl...
Could have been a debutante
in Jack and Jill.
Might have been class president —
dreams to fulfill...
but no dance with my father.

I walked those streets alone with just one plea —
that some sweet song of hope
might play for me...
that some sweet hour of prayer
might set me free.

Daddy's little angel —
but no dance with my father.
No lessons on being loved...
no memory of loving partners...
no witness to the Lord above —
only abuse, incest and regret.

I walked those streets; my body's not my own.
Sold on shelves of shame and racks of greed.
needle track tattoos adorn my arms,
evidence of the demons,
that won this fight.

Amiri's Time

the game has changed.
young black poets try to swing so hard...
try to throw down so hard.
lyrics of fury and such—
but the old-heads remember...
and they say,
he was the incubator
for unapologetic blackness.
changed his name
and flipped the game—
before the new jacks
were even notions
of hip-hop hyperbole
and spoken word slams
in the distended bellies
of 2-young-2-be pregnant
brown-skinned mamas.
never safe, nor sanitized,
his imagery defiantly tantalized—
and brutalized...
and cauterized...
the open wounds
of slavery's past, and
all the negroes who wouldn't last
with an ongoing slave's mentality.
imagery that startled the white man...
verses that spoke of a black-skinned plan.
nothin' a dude named LeRoi could say...
imagery of a chocolate day
of deliverance,
far too malevolent
for white folks' digestion.
caucasians that remember,
may even breathe
a sigh of relief today.
'cause such an intense brother,
who spoke out against

other brothers
"who sometimes killed each other"
and who sometimes "failed to walk the air",
has closed his own soul's window.
he no longer looks down
on the dirty courtyard
we call america.

For Amiri Baraka, RIP
January 9, 2014

—RIFFS—

"Until the lions have their historians, tales of the hunt
shall always favor the hunter."

UGANDAN PROVERB

Cell Phone Nation

I'm never alone.
I got a cell phone.
Standin' in the grocery line,
yes, you hear me carp and whine.
I don't have to hold my tongue.
Doesn't matter, old or young...
I refuse to be alone,
long as I got my mobile phone.

I flip the lid
and get to yakkin'.
What of the looks
that I'm attracting.
Yeah I'm loud and boisterous too.
Me and my celly
don't care about you.

On the bus or in a crowd —
hear my laughter.
Heck, I'm proud.
You think it's wrong or rude of me,
to trash this new technology.
But I don't have to be alone.
There's minutes left on this here phone.

It's not just me.
Man, look around...
This whole darn nation's
star and pound...
Blackberry, I-phone, Android, too...
Old folks squawkin' like the young ones do.
No one has to be alone,
as long as they got a plan and a phone.

It's dumbin' down society.
We need cell phone sobriety.
Your business broadcast in 4G —

Where's your sense of modesty?
The death of all civility
on Sprint, Nextel and ATT.
Crazy ringtones always jinglin'
can't tell whose, they're always minglin'.

I may not even like the guy.
Don't matter, I still signify.
My gadget fix just gets me high—
and I don't need no alibi.
All the while I see you cringing,
while I'm lost in two-way binging.
Face it chief, I'm in the zone.
No dropped calls on my cell phone.

Down Goes Frazier

Smokin' Joe and the Louisville Lip—
One a savant, ultra-cool and hip...
One blue collar, determined and strong...
One good and pretty, the other dead wrong.

Three great fights for a legacy—
But all the acclaim went to Mr. Ali.
In the heart of Philly, Joe's home town,
Rocky got love, but no love for dark brown.

He beat the man at MSG.
But the Garden's man he'd never be.
Muhammad called him "Tom" and "Gorilla".
through their epic war in the heart of Manila.

Joe won Olympic gold for us too.
But Frazier was never the man we knew.
Joe was the one that history threw,
out of the plane that Cassius flew.

Ali proclaimed "The Champ is Here!"
Still, Frazier's gifts were just as clear.
A prodding brute with lethal intent,
his hands of stone were like cement.

He beat the guys that Ali fought.
He was never bossed and never bought.
The "pretty one's" smile mocked Frazier's frown.
Muhammad's ascent took Frazier down.

Smokin' Joe and the Louisville Lip—
One who mastered the ego trip...
One content to valiantly fight—
then move to shadowy corners of night.

Facebook Post #5 (for Maya Naomi)

When you were little (just a wee thing), you used to love to

dance on my feet,

to Lena Horne singing "Stormy Weather"

or any other juicy jazz ballad that I'd play on the stereo.

Music and dance are in your spirit like piano keys

under the Duke's fingers,

or poetry on Maya Angelou's lips...

You are ever the daughter-muse to a poet-father,

the daughter-muse to a dancer-mother,

the spirit feather that tickles the fancy of a laughing God!

Blessings dear one...

—Poppy Tee—

Livin' Out Loud

New York sisters live out loud—
never afraid to be black and proud,
won't get lost in the madding crowd,
impassioned, embattled,
but never bowed.

Songbird Jill said,
"Queens shouldn't swing."
But to chicks from Brooklyn,
it ain't no thing.
Always down for the physical fling...
first out the whip,
when they hear the bell ring.

I remember Roni from Co-op City.
Sweet, petit, and oh-so pretty—
but tougher than leather
and twice as gritty...
Down for whatever,
like Ness and Nitty.

'Round the way girls
are big-time fighters,
ride-or-die chicks and
Saturday nighters.
Bed-Stuy, Hollis, and a few
Crown Heighters.
Original G's, but never biters.

Bachata to hip-hop—
game-changers...
wary of punks, pimps, and strangers,
hip to the jungle's cruel dangers—
like hustlers,
thugs, and gang-bangers.

Frosty, like mid-February—

Funny like Tom and like Jerry
Fresh as a ripe black cherry
Flame on, incendiary.

Apple attitudes, fully intact—
dynamic divas and that's a fact,
your faulty game cannot attract...
My brother, she ain't calling back.

Curvy butts in Apple Bottoms...
tattoos, yeah, they probably got 'em.
Five earrings on each tan lobe...
fingernails done with a map of the globe.
The style you may refute.
The stance you must salute.

New York girls don't whisper!
They live out loud, my sister.
Make sure you haven't dissed her...
on facebook, or on Twitter.

They're never lost in the madding crowd—
They're not afraid to be black and proud.
Impassioned, empowered, and never bowed...
New York sisters live out loud.

Shale

He wasn't live, in color—
But he wasn't black and white.
His hair was kind of kinky.
And he wore his shades at night.

Yeah, he lacked some pigment.
His skin was strangely pale.
But he acted like a brother.
So we just called him Shale.

A move or two in rhythm—
was all that he could muster.
Still homeboy wasn't bigoted,
a cracker, or a buster.

It made the brothers wonder—
what was his Holy Grail?
A Norseman's frozen tundra,
or chicken in a paper pail.

He'd brush his teeth to Dr. Dre,
and ate his grits with shrimp.
But he knew the truth, the life, the way—
and never tried to pimp.

Dude's cool with Crips and convicts—
though he's never been to jail.
He blogs 'bout drugs, and guns and gangs—
a slave set-up, that's doomed to fail.

He's got a few white friends...
but they seldom get his vibe.
The Ivy Leagues all chased him—
as a scholar and a scribe.

Still Watts, Detroit, and Harlem,
all made him feel alive.

He could have gone white collar—
but it lacked the jazz and jive.

Was he passing for a brother—
bi-racial, albino, or strangely pale?
Hey, he acted like a brother.
So we just called him Shale.

Old School Jam (Act Like You Heard!)

Yo my mellow, don't you hear?
Old school's in the atmosphere.
Yo my mellow, ain't it clear?
Like a pack of Kools and a High Life beer.

Godfather's havin' a funky good time,
glistenin' with sweat and that Conkoline shine.
Maceo's horns, Fred Wesley too...
down-home brothers, just doin' the do.

Can't you feel the bass line hit?
Old school rhythms, killin' it.

All together, live, uncut—
Old school made you shake your butt.
The newest dances, every week,
Soul Train lines on every street.

Ohio Players meet Kool & the Gang.
You know Aretha wants to hang.
Tempts, Dramatics, Spinners, and Tops,
rent party, somebody called the cops.
Colored folks will act a' fool—
whenever the dee-jay is spinnin' old school.

Can't you feel the bass line hit?
Old school rhythms, killin' it.

One of those nights
when you want to get down
with that Go-go beat,
just play Chuck Brown.
Heatwave's 'bout to set it off right,
while Tower of Power blows
through the night.

That old school flavor—
you getting'this , boss?
Like chicken wings
and Frank's hot sauce.

Delphonics, La-La Means I Love..,
Earth, Wind, & Fire lookin' above,
sing "Keep Your Head to the Sky"...
Neo-soul-new-jacks don't even try.

Classic music, all night long...
Real folk, rockin' my favorite song.
Don't you remember the New York Rocker?
Didn't you groove to Frankie Crocker?
The first brotherman on VH-1...
then found Jesus before he was done.
Classic music all night long...
Real folk, rockin' my favorite song.

Can't you feel the bass line hit?
Old school rhythms, killin' it.

Parliament, so Funkadelic—
that kind of jam is almost a relic.
Mandrill's Fencewalk and Ape is High...
Pleasure's Joyous, my, my, my!
Slave, and Brick, and Brass Construction,
Maze and don't forget Confunkshun.

Hollywood even gave old-school a try,
with Shaft, the Mack, and Superfly.
Curtis Mayfield and Isaac Hayes,
and Willie Hutch's funky ways.
Brother's Gonna' Work It Out.
Sister's gave that old school shout.

Phyllis Hyman and 'Berta Flack,
almost gave brothers a heart attack...
So much emotion and so much soul—
melting wax in your honey's ear hole.

Grandmaster Flash and the Furious Five,
White Lines dropped like an angry beehive.
Put the lyrics all up in your face,
takin' rap to a whole new place.

Jam Master Jay with original hip-hop...
scratchin' and cuttin' and rhymes, non-stop.

Adidas gear, from head-to-toe—
rockin' that Hollis, Queens-y flow.

Chuck D., Dre, and KRS-1...
takin' the game out into the sun.
Look to impact hip-hop proper,
edutainin' the sho'nuff show-stopper.
Sad to say, Tupac was done...
before his fame was truly won.
But now true hip-hop sings his praises,
while new gees try to bite his phrases.

Music was the message then...
wish we'd get it back again.
No Stevie Wonder's,
No Luther or Marvin,
Hathaway's gone.
Real soul is starvin'.

Yet loud and clear,
on the high-tech tip...
like a thumpin' beat,
in a shiny whip—
the Old school story is on and poppin',
like nana's gravy and biscuit soppin'.

Yo my mellows, can't you hear?
Pandora's streaming, loud and clear.
Funkin' for real—you make the choice.
Old school jams—new high-def voice...
Sirius satellite radio heaven...
soul food classics, 24-7.
XM's got the funk on lock.
You can hear the bass,
clear 'round the block.

Old school music never dies...
Like Be-Be's kids, it multiplies.

TMI – Too Much Information

All your pics for the world to see—
is that the way it's s'posed to be?
All your business in graphics and type…
too much reality, too much hype.

Your showing your tats and piercings too.
in places you ought to keep, just to you.
Turning your "friends" into peeps and voyeurs—
Thicke said the lines are incredibly blurred.

The too small bikinis, your booty in thongs—
you tweet everybody your favorite sex songs…
You tell on your partners and hint at details
of hook-ups you're planning when true love fails.

Flossin' on facebook and frontin' on Twitter—
draggin' your dirt like kitties in litter…
Mad at the haters your postings create,
hoping the scandals will soon dissipate.

4COL—what's with your generation?
LMBO—at your boo's situation…
SMH—that's some wild deviation…
TMI— that's too much information.

Tyson–The Titan Deconstructed

Manchild, Brooklyn-born…
excesses of anger, hate, and scorn.
Becalmed by D'Amato's steady hand—
a fatherly figure and a tight-knit band.
A family…
No hangers-on or sycophants,
no fight-club ho's with breast implants…
just running and training to army chants.
Fighting all comers, class by class,
KO's come easy, he's brutal and fast.

The feeble challengers fell at his feet…
crumpled in a vanquished heap.
One after another after another.
Helpless against the body shots,
the hooks and jabs and seeing spots.
Little canaries circling their hazy heads—
like Loony Tunes loosed
from matinee afternoons.

Then in an instant, Cus was gone.
The brooding titan was set upon.
Soon the barbarians,
assaulted the gates
and killed the palace guards.

Cultivating strange appetites,
destructive days and manic nights.
steroidal rage and depression—
Like a lion in a shrinking cage,
sexual aggression…
no disciplined repression…
becomes a cruel obsession.

Then a woman with wiles
and secret aims—
envelopes the manchild,

with self-centered games.
Uses, abuses and refuses,
to be the good wife.
Becoming just a day
in the life
of a titan's sure demise.

A King with a gangster's pedigree,
perched like a vulture his chance to see—
then pounced and feigned father-love.
The wild-haired scoundrel with
sinister aims—
steals and destroys, or just maims.
Same thing...
Opened scars that hadn't healed,
bloody abrasions not yet repealed...
the ways that the germs get in...
fights he could never win.

Nights of drugs, debauchery—
years in lock-up, 1-2-3...
sexual brutality,
victim and villain, alternately.

So the end result becomes quite clear.
The warring spirit admits to fear.
And a Buster beats the brawler up,
on a faraway island with Asian shores.
There, the untimely demise
dawns with the red sunrise.
The mighty young titan,
was never the same.
His power and speed
and the soul of his game—
were gone.

A meal ticket and a running joke,
bizarre tattoos and nearly broke...
Beyond the millions made,
the millions spent...

the demons came—
collecting rent,
and the deathly wages of sin.

The titan deconstructed—
no redemptive forgiving graces,
just pitying looks, or angry faces.
Unlike the G.O.A.T., the greatest, Ali...
broken down, beaten up, permanently.
The butt of bad jokes on cable TV.
A character for the cineplex
boxing's young titan—
sweet science's "ex".

Iron Mike, narrator, tragically-flawed.
Once steel-fisted, now strangely de-clawed...
No longer legend, or pound-for-pound...
No longer mythic, Prometheus unbound...
No longer, most dangerous man on the planet...
No longer chiseled from a block of brown granite.

Just a 12-step bum with a curious tale—
a prison lifer, in and out of jail...
destined to dominate,
only to fail.

Iron Mike Tyson—
deconstructed...
Even titans fall—
when a white-hot iron,
can't find an anvil,
a proofing fire,
and a worthy smith.

The sharpest blade
can be unmade.

My Whip Is Fly!

Runnin' from the tax man,
'cause my bill's so high…
I may be tore up from the floor up—
but my whip is fly.

22's and spinners, solid chrome, reflect the sky.
Peepin' all the haters as I roll on by.
Got a honey in the bucket, say she'll ride or die.
I know she's just flossin', 'cause my whip is fly.

Can't pay back the money' you lent.
And I ain't got the paper to meet my rent.
But I bought new mats at the auto supply…
My pockets are empty, but my whip is fly.

Two miles an hour so everybody sees me—
simonized and detailed, so homeys want to be me.
You can't help starin', so don't even try…
There ain't no comparin'; umph, my whip is fly.

Chrysler 300 with the big chrome grill…
lookin' like a Bentley comin' down the hill.
Some women think I'm ugly…I ain't got no alibi.
Still they try to jock me, 'cause my whip is fly.

Got the leather seats and the cherry console…
DVD player and remote control.
Can I get a couple dollars, 'cause my tank's bone dry?
I'm too darn broke, for a whip this fly.

My situation ain't even cool…
My mama thinks I'm a daggone fool.
My note's five hunnert and insurance is high…
But you can't hate a brother with a whip this fly.

Bose CD with the I-Pod connection—
thumpin' that bass in every direction.

Windows ease down when I ease on by...
I must be pimpin' with a whip so fly.

Two-tone paint, smoke silver and blue...
Check out your teeth, grinnin' back at you.
What can you say, except, "my, my, my..."
I know I got some issues, but my whip is fly.

—DATE NIGHT—

"When one is in love, a cliff becomes a meadow."

ETHIOPIAN PROVERB

Chocolate Uncovered

I will keep this memory for myself.
Not like a sip of Coke and a smile—
not like my swag, my street cred, my style...
but a fondness for sweets, I've had for a while.

I won't tell this tale in the locker room.
Where the boys expose their nasty side,
boasting of "hook-ups", with lustful pride.
One doesn't speak thusly of his bride.

Still a hint I'll give of your perfect grace.
God favored me so overmuch—
to let me feel your loving touch.
Men call me lucky, such and such.

You are the straw that stirs my drink.
Subtle, exotic and rich to the blood—
the river that makes my passions flood...
the rose that blooms from a lush, green bud.

I'm captured by your ebony soul's
bubblin' brown sugar audacity...
chocolate frosted intensity—
chocolate uncovered, but only for me.

I'm a captive of your mystery...
Not knowing how you'll surprise—
a natural ability to mesmerize,
with wisdom that flows in your ebony eyes.

I will keep this memory for myself.
Not like a sip of champagne from a slipper...
not like I'm anxious to undo your zipper,
but like sweet nectar drawn by a bronze honey dipper.

Daddy

My baby girl, she tells me—
all the time, in fact…
Daddy I do love you, and
between us there's a pact…
to never let a hateful world
keep us from each other,
to always keep our family strong—
you and me, and mother.

She says, I see it all the time,
with every passing day—
lonely girls with broken hearts,
whose dads have gone away.
Absent, dead, incarcerated,
livin' on the low…
druggin', or intoxicated,
no good seeds to sow.

I see it when I ride the trains.
Each week the gangs get larger.
Angry boys with pent up rage,
who never knew a father.
Their attitudes and nastiness,
each day, they just grow bigger
They treat each other shamefully—
and use that foul word, n*****.

But in the things you taught, I trust
these heathens will not get me.
Though heaven knows wherever I go,
they always try to sweat me.
Their gangster chicks, say "ride or die…"
and steady try to hang.
Profane raps, and backward caps—
they've also multiplied.

I see them in the shopping mall,
carriages in tow.
Babies made by baby girls...
Winter, Spring and Fall.
No more time for classes,
college plans destroyed—
gave up all their assets,
just to get some boy.

Just to get some street-wise dude,
sagging jeans and tats—
smokin' blunts and chasin' butt...
jumpin' ship like rats.
Not a one was raised like you—
raised to be a man...
raised with God and family,
central to the plan.

My baby girl she tells me this...
and much more still, she writes.
I want to always feel the love,
that tucks me in at night.
Ours, a bond of hope and trust,
that some girls never had.
I'll always cherish what it means,
to call you simply, "Dad."

Dedicated to my beloved daughter, Maya Naomi
Spring, 2012

Prelude to a Kiss

The hopeful glance
from across the room—
adrift in the air,
like dust from a broom.
Not quite romance,
but promising...
the chance that hope
had gifts to bring.

The stars aloft
in the evening sky—
you looked up,
and so did I.
Twinkling beads
of magic light,
danced against
the veil of night.

Beckoned by
the need for love—
who would doubt
the signs above?
Who would fail,
to take this chance?
Dreams, would you
care to dance?

Inching toward
inviting lips,
a tingle in
your fingertips...
Who could fault
the rhyme of this—
a prelude to
a kiss.

The mood was bright
with passion's glow—
rushing us toward
the undertow.
Now reason warns you,
"just say no."
But your spirit's compass
made you go.

The music filled
our ears like wine...
intoxicating,
and divine.
My eyes met yours,
in three/four time...
as rhythm twirled
to greet the rhyme.

What makes longing,
linger thusly?
Now conceding,
you can trust me...
Beckoned by
the need for love—
who could doubt
the circling dove.

Your glance—
a prelude to a kiss...
Slumber wakes
to all of this.
Not quite romance,
but promising...
the chance that hope,
has gifts to bring.

Pretty Brown Girl

Gonna' fall in love again today...
not something I thought I needed to do.
She's my boo already and my bestie too.
But here's the thing...
She's a pretty brown girl,
with big brown eyes
and a sexy nose.
Man she's chocolate candy,
from her head to her toes.
She's my brown spice of life.
She's my brown beans and rice.
She's my brown, pretty wife.
So I'm 'bout to do it again today...
Seems like there's just no other way...
What can a brother really say?
Except—she's a pretty brown girl.
Got it from her mama,
fine like Michelle Obama.
Fine without the drama,
you sometimes get with beauty,
that's only skin deep.
But I don't have that issue.
She's pretty to the bone,
with that chocolate undertone...
Puts a brother in the zone—
just can't leave the girl alone.
Just can't help myself,
from falling in love again,
like I seem to do each day.
Not something I anticipate,
though still I must appreciate...
Okay, that's it, I'm runnin' late.
You see, I got this weekly date—
with my bestie and my boo.
By now, you know her too.
She's right over there...
She's the pretty brown girl.

Black Love, White Romance

Ours is the agony of slaves torn asunder—
the rape by the master and sexual plunder...
How love survives, we are all made to wonder.

Ours is the stain of incarceration—
millions of brothers, a virtual nation...
millions of sisters in search of salvation.

The frenzied cries to the heavens above—
these are the sad songs, lost in black love.

Theirs is the white steed with flowing mane—
The knight in bright armor who rides through the rain...
two lovers, breathlessly, meet on the plain.

Theirs is the princess of long blonde locks—
Dowries of crown jewels, mansions, and stocks...
nightly Manhattans, chilled on the rocks.

The wistful sigh and the knowing glance—
these are the trappings of white romance.

Ours is the child without a last name—
The hood, and the corner, and playing the game...
the hustle for money, the lack of true shame.

Ours is the sister who followed the line—
Fell into the life and the pimp's cruel design...
lost on the streets, no longer to shine.

The shattering grip of the ghetto's glove—
these are demons that shadow black love.

Theirs is the coed with beauty and brains—
The Ivy League grad from the Midwestern plains...
who marries the banker for capital gains.

Theirs are the kids who inherit the lot.
Theirs is the condo, the nanny, the yacht.
Theirs is the status that old money bought.

The couple that summers in Southern France—
these are the riches of white romance.

Ours is the church at the top of the hill.
Ours is the hope that fear cannot kill.
Ours is a bond with the Father's good will.

Ours is the mama that nurtures the dream.
Ours is the papa that sows by the stream.
Ours is a village that calls itself team.

The faith of our fathers, flies like the dove.
This is the promise of righteous black love.

Theirs is a trophy-wife, socialite heir—
not so bright, but blonde and fair...
model physique and a clueless stare.

Theirs is the maid he snuck through the back—
the cocaine he bought in the shotgun shack...
his pre-nup agreement that takes it all back.

The counseling visits that never succeed—
this is a white romance in need.

Ours is the small home, no deck and no pool—
where the kids all want to hang out after school,
the Christian parents who just seem cool.

Ours is the daddy who reads us stories—
of brown-skinned heroes and all their glories...
of parables and allegories.

The blessings that fall from heaven above—
these are the showers that fall on black love.

Sub-ways #1

They entered the train at the very first stop.
They jockeyed to sit at their favorite spot.
Coveted corner seats, right at the door—
backpack and tote bag then placed on the floor.

I watched the two of them, coupled up clearly—
She wore a ring, for which he paid dearly.
Both of them business-like, sensible shoes...
world-worn travelers, Monday morn blues.

She with her Kindle reading intently—
he with an I-Pad, screen touching gently.
After some distance they came to her stop.
She pecked at his cheek, no crackle or pop.

Is this the ride they were bound to take?
All widgets and gadgets and mostly fake...
Slaves to the things that strangers built—
motley squares on a thread-bare quilt.

Are these the lives they were destined to lead?
Not to relate, but to withdraw and read...
The train moves on steadily under the streets.
And mannequins might as well sit on the seats.

Witnessing daily, these "sub-ways," we're shown,
our brothers concerns are never our own.
Even the lovers with mutual cares,
flee from the scene for their separate affairs.

A subway saga unfolds each day,
as less and less attention we pay...
to the souls whose space we rush to share—
with shaded glances and cold, blank stares.

Sub-ways #2

This ride seems more sublime than another—
as they ride the rails, one sister, one brother.
A kinship of glances, of smiles and nods,
suggests a connection that nature prods.

The metal clad coaches glide down the rails.
And slowly emotions come out of their jails.
Their eyes dance boldly through each squeal and hiss,
imagining the sweetness of an unknown kiss.

Perhaps they long for relationships—
entangled hearts and fingertips.
Perhaps they only fantasize,
of steamy nights and heaving thighs.

Longing to connect, he thinks
of clever banter and furtive winks—
of stolen lust for a sinful wage.
Perhaps she's got a facebook page.

Romancing the notion of passionate eyes,
they come to their stop and quickly rise.
Maybe tomorrow, he'll see her again.
She wonders if, he'll speak to her then.

Is this the ride that has to be—
a lover's tale we never see?
Faces emerge from a snip of sleep,
shocked by the lurch of schedules to keep.

Sister, When Do You Get Off?

You waited on my table
and served me with a smile.
I tried to keep it super-cool—
But still, I liked your style.

Your walk was one of dignity,
despite your working station.
I had to calm the thought I had
to ply you with temptation.

I finally caught your glance again
with a made-up little cough.
I blurted out the question, "Sister,
when do you get off?"

You kind of looked me up and down—
but never went off script.
Describing dinner specials,
while I gulped and bit my lip.

And then you asked a question,
to which I could respond.
"Brother, are you saved?" you asked.
I said, "Is Mae West blonde?"

You smiled again and then you laughed.
Your aura was engaging.
I prayed that you'd discern the true—
faith campaign I was waging.

Your eyes met mine, but cautiously...
And then you whispered this—
"The evening soups are minestrone,
and spicy lobster bisque."

I must admit, the cool in you
was working all my nerves—
Messing with my poet's flow,
my adjectives, and my verbs.

I finally found my grown man voice,
and ordered Sea Bass Grill.
You seemed to like my dinner choice—
rosemary, sage, and dill.

Sensing less resistance, I asked about your church.
Warming to this inquiry, you said, "I go to Birch."
"Birchwood Temple, on the hill?" I was a bit surprised.
"I pray there every Tuesday morning, just about sunrise."

"Morning prayer," that's really great,
you said with affirmation.
Then you said one other thing,
that shook my faith foundation.

"I'd really like to talk with you,
beyond this four course meal—
But messed-up past relationships
left scars that just won't heal."

"What could be that story?
Your smile, it never fades."
"I hide my problem pretty well—
But brother, I've got AIDS."

I felt the tightening in my chest,
and hoped she'd miss my gasp of breath.
She clearly saw I was a wreck.
She quickly said "I'll get your check."

The very soul of ministry,
was testing me that day.
I took her hand and asked her,
"Can we meet at Birch to pray?"

That was the beginning.
We've been married now two years.
Souls witnessed to His winning,
been through health concerns and fears.

Clear-eyed and in covenant,
we've challenges to face.
But God grants us serenity,
and lends His matchless grace.

I made my mind up even then.
To her I pledged my troth.
I ask her now on date night, "Sister,
when do you get off?"

To Say What I Saw

It's gonna be hard for a man to describe...
But a brother won't need to take a bribe,
to say what I saw
when I first saw your face.

Perhaps it won't roll gently off my tongue,
like a poet's boast, all prideful and young...
Still, I'll say what I saw
when I came to this place.

Your radiance shone like a sun-kissed morn—
the honied gold of sweet August corn.
The angels clapped on the day you were born.
And the trumpet player blew his horn.
Melody danced.
Harmony pranced.
Rhythm advanced.
On the day you were born.

The gentle elegance of your gait,
made women stop, then look, then hate.
Made busy brothers hesitate.
Made busy brothers very late.
Made busy brothers miss the gate.
Made busy brothers watch and wait.

The moon dipped low to kiss your smile.
The stars lined up for many a mile.
The scribes wrote volumes about your style.
I stood there dumbstruck all the while.

Like Roberta Flack's haunting melody,
the gifts you brought made blind men see.
To the dark, endless skies they return each night...
'til the end of time, resplendent and bright.

To say what I saw
when I first saw your face—
is to live forever embracing a dream
of a love so much finer than any could seem.

To say what I saw
is forever revealing,
and never concealing
the huge butterflies
my stomach is dealing, dealing, dealing—
with right now...

as I try to say—
what I saw,
when I first saw you face.

Dedicated to my beloved wife and life partner, Terésa... the butterflies still flutter wildly!

CPSIA information can be obtained at www.ICGtesting.com
Printed in the USA
BVOW02s1438020514

352313BV00001B/5/P

9 781629 524740